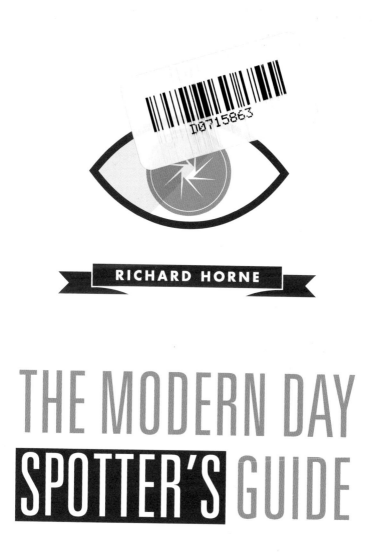

RICHARD HORNE

THE MODERN DAY
SPOTTER'S GUIDE

FOR

HELEN, MARLIE & LUKAS

SQUARE PEG London.
Published by Square Peg 2013

2   4   6   8   10   9   7   5   3   1

Text and design and illustration copyright © Richard Horne 2013. The author has asserted his right under the Copyright, Designs and Patents Act 1988 to be identified as the author of this work. This book is sold subject to the condition that it shall not, by way of trade or otherwise, be lent, resold, hired out, or otherwise circulated without the publisher's prior consent in any form of binding or cover other than that in which it is published and without a similar condition, including this condition, being imposed on the subsequent purchaser.

First published in Great Britain in 2013 by Square Peg Random House, 20 Vauxhall Bridge Road, London SW1V 2SA. www.vintage-books.co.uk Addresses for companies within The Random House Group Limited can be found at: www.randomhouse.co.uk/offices.htm The Random House Group Limited Reg. No. 954009. A CIP catalogue record for this book is available from the British Library. ISBN 97802 240 95518.

The Random House Group Limited supports the Forest Stewardship Council®(FSC®), the leading international forest-certification organisation.Our books carrying the FSC label are printed on FSC®-certified paper. FSC is the only forest-certification scheme supported by the leading environmental organisations,including Greenpeace. Our paper procurement policy can be found at www.randomhouse.co.uk/environment. Printed and bound in China by C&C Offset Printing Co., Ltd.

MIX
Paper from
responsible sources
FSC® C008047
FSC
www.fsc.org

THIS BOOK BELONGS TO

INTRODUCTION

Unusual, uplifting and downright ridiculous events are happening all the time, and may easily be missed as you journey through your familiar surroundings as part of the daily grind. By taking a closer look at the environment around you, you'll hopefully spot something that's worth sharing. It might be something that makes you laugh or smile, groan or sigh; it might prompt you to do something you wouldn't normally do, or change the way you think. *The Modern Day Spotter's Guide* is a way to chart and celebrate these often fleeting but noteworthy moments.

In this book you'll find categories to cover all aspects of modern life, from the media and transport, to nature, animals and, of course, those most fascinating of creatures, people. With a little help from those you know, as well as hundreds you don't, you'll be able to achieve many of the sightings mentioned in this guide, as your fly-on-the-wall lens allows you to observe a glorious array of unique habits, strange quirks, varied routines and accidental escapades.

Research for *The Modern Day Spotter's Guide* has been ongoing my whole life. The list was compiled using sightings and stories documented from the day-to-day world around me. On telling others about the idea for the book, I found that they had also borne witness to things that helped shape the list. For instance, I heard a lot of stories about seeing *something left on the roof of a car* (No. 1). A friend's mum once left the frozen Christmas turkey on the roof of her car, driving all the way home while it slowly defrosted in the breeze. Soon after hearing this story, I met another friend who had just become the owner of a new pair of gloves that had fallen at her feet after being jettisoned from the roof of a car that sped past.

The general public have also inspired me over the years, offering a daily serving of interesting and amusing insights into the numerous peculiarities of our species ... but it hasn't all been one-way traffic. If you take a little something you should give a little something back and, unfortunately for me, I have participated in some embarrassing mishaps on far too many occasions, some of which I won't be mentioning here.

Among the stories I am willing to share is the time I once strode confidently down the street wearing a pair of the newest and bluest jeans around, worn on the day were bought, so new, in fact, that the long white size stickers on the backs of the legs could be seen far and wide as the sunlight hit them on the two-mile walk into work. This embarrassing moment went on to inspire *Spot a wardrobe malfunction* (No. 13).

When it comes to amusing accidents, the time I planned a scene-stealing entrance on my BMX backfired spectacularly when a perfectly timed snapping of the brake cable sent me and the bike cruising, at speed, straight into the lake my mates were meeting by. Thankfully for me, this was a time just before every member of society had a smart phone permanently in front of their face to capture my *epic fail* (No. 70). If this incident were to happen tomorrow, then you can bet my foolish antics would be uploaded to YouTube and shared on Facebook and Twitter within minutes, immortalising my humiliation for ever.

This tale is a perfect example of schadenfreude. Schadenfreude is a German word that simply means 'harm' and 'joy', and roughly translates as gaining pleasure from someone else's misfortune. I've been subject to a lot of schaden in my time on this planet so far, but I've also had my fair share of freude too. So be prepared to participate in, as well witness, the things in this book. Whether it be coincidence, accident, stupidity or nature that plays the storymaker, the protoganist could very easily be you.

Above all, the idea is to have fun. To appreciate life's rich tapestry and enliven the apparently dull and ordinary. To come away with an armful of anecdotes and a wealth of experience. It is not about laughing at the misfortune of others, but about being able to laugh at ourselves and our futile struggle for dignity when nature, events and situations spiral out of our control. We are all in this together, after all.

HOW TO USE THE BOOK

Events worth spotting and jotting rarely come with an advance warning, so try to be prepared for the unexpected. Familiarise yourself with the seventy spots listed in this book. The pages have been prepared for you to quickly document what you saw, where and when it happened and, if possible, how or why on earth it did.

SPOTS

Don't take the title of each spot too literally. The list has been chosen for you to have fun with, and where you see underlined lighter text in the title of a spot, feel free to substitute those words with something different, something you have seen, as shown below.

See the face of _Elvis Presley_ in _A pineapple slice_

....

In the example opposite, for instance, *See the face of Jesus in your soup* (No. 4), there's no need to disregard other famous cameos as you eat. Tom Cruise, Michael Jackson or Napoleon will all do just as nicely. Nor should you spend the rest of your life eating only soup. Keep an eye out for famous faces hiding in tomatoes, slices of salami, melted cheese and burned toast. If a food or drink product can form a well-known face, then you'll have a valid spot.

There is potential for crossover between some spots in this list, but the idea is to see as wide and interesting a variety of incidents as possible. So if you do see something that could be categorised in more than one way, please choose the spot that best fits and look out for something a bit different in nature for the other one.

For example, if you really were to see the face of Tom Cruise in your slice of salami, it would be a valid entry for either the *face in an everyday place* spot (No. 29) or the *face of Jesus in your soup* spot. However, as it fits the criteria of the second one more precisely, that would be the best place for it, and you can have fun trying to find an altogether different kind of face for the *everyday place* spot.

SEE

If something mentioned in *The Modern Day Spotter's Guide* should happen before your eyes, try to record the moment with a drawing or photograph that encapsulates the incident in a nutshell and stick this in your witness report, as shown in the example on the next page. Hopefully you'll have the necessary equipment to hand during a spotting episode (see **WHAT YOU NEED**, p. xv), but if you don't happen to have either a camera or this book with you, make a mental note of as many of the details of the event as you can, and fill out your witness report at the earliest opportunity.

Spot a face in an everyday place

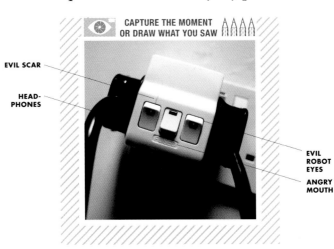

CAPTURE THE MOMENT
OR DRAW WHAT YOU SAW

EVIL SCAR

HEAD-
PHONES

EVIL
ROBOT
EYES

ANGRY
MOUTH

WITNESS REPORT

Your witness reports can be as detailed as you like. In some cases, a single photo or drawing may be enough. There are some reports that ask for more information, encouraging you to record what you saw by answering simple questions about the event. There is always a space on the right to log any other details you wish to remember.

Here is a glossary of some of the infographics you may come across in these report forms. Sometimes you will need to tick more than one:

Who did this involve?

Male   Pensioner(s)   Toddler   Work   Friend(s)   Pet(s)/   An
                                   colleague(s) or family   animal(s) object
     Female   Kid(s)   Baby   Stranger(s)   Youth(s)   A   Other
                                                                 vehicle

POINTS

A points system has been designed to challenge you to go for the better or rarer spots, and to encourage you to share and compete with other known Modern Day Spotters. Depending on the precise nature of your spot, you can earn 5, 10, 15 or 20 points, and you can tick more than one option as applicable. For example:

See someone's double

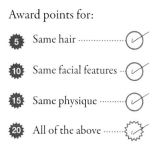

Award points for:

5 Same hair

10 Same facial features

15 Same physique

20 All of the above

If you end up ticking all the boxes, award yourself the grand total of 50 points. In the example shown, 20 points are given for doing 'All the above', but that still means you get a grand total of 50 points.

$$5 + 10 + 15 + 20 = \mathbf{50} \text{ points}$$

TASK

For an extra 25 or 50 bonus points, try to complete the accompanying task for each spot. Here is the task for *See someone's double* (No. 52):

On the right-hand page, at the bottom of the form, you can record your results for the task. You will generally be able to award yourself 25 points for giving the task a go, but 50 points are available for accomplishing the task with flair:

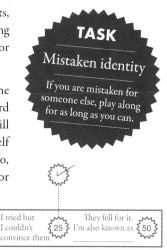

TASK

Mistaken identity

If you are mistaken for someone else, play along for as long as you can.

| **TASK** Mistaken identity | I tried but I couldn't convince them | **25** | They fell for it. I'm also known as | **50** |

FINAL TOTALS

Once you've witnessed one of the spots in the book, and filled out the relevant form, enter your combined score in the **YOUR TOTALS** pages at the back. Do this each time you complete a spot, and remember to keep a note of the date you completed it too.

| 52 | 12 10 13 | See someone's double | 75 |

SHARE AND SHARE ALIKE

If you think your spot deserves to be shared, upload it to the *Modern Day Spotter's Guide* website: www.spottersguide.co.uk or the facebook page: www.facebook.com/theMDSGbook.

WHAT YOU NEED

A sharp pair of eyes. If your eyesight is a little lacking, glasses, contact lenses, magnifying glasses and binoculars (used with discretion) are also acceptable tools in your hunt for the perfect spot.

A camera or smart phone. These items are essential for capturing a lasting record of your spots, be they interestingly shaped objects, mis-spelled signage or mysterious and amusing behaviour.

Stationery. If you don't have the book to hand, write down what you see immediately with the help of paper, pens or pencils. The longer you take to write it down, the more detail you may forget. If a camera is unavailable, draw what you see with these implements.

Members of the public, nature and inanimate objects. Now that you're ready to start spotting, you just need to wait for your star performers to appear.

THE LIST

1. Spot something left on the roof of a car

2. Spot an escaped animal

3. Spot an unusual-shaped cloud

4. See the face of Jesus in your soup

5. Spot a commuter miss their stop

6. Spot an amusing place name

7. Spot a photo bombing

8. Spot a movie mistake

9. Spot a wild animal using public transport

10. Spot a modern-day shooting star

11. Spot someone in a time warp

12. Spot a living statue on a break

13. Spot a wardrobe malfunction

14. Spot an invisible foe attack

15. Spot someone using unusual transport

16. Spot an amusing news headline

17. Spot a thieving seagull

18. Spot an embarrassed parent

19. See your name on a gravestone

20. Spot a dancing plastic bag

21. Spot an awkward date

22. Spot an amusingly shaped vegetable

23. Spot an amusing auto-correction

24. Spot something unusual on a bus shelter

25. Spot a public typo

26. Spot a food malfunction

27. Spot interesting facial hair

28. Spot a celebrity lookalike

29. See a face in an everyday place

30. Spot a competitive parent

31. Spot something unusual on Google Street View

32. Spot a bird-poo victim

33. Spot a dropped photo

34. Spot someone with techno rage

35. Spot an inappropriate T-shirt

36. Spot a pigeon with one foot

37. Spot a battle against the wind

38. Spot a prank

39. Spot something you've dreamt about

40. Spot a bad hair day

41. Spot a good deed

42. Spot the inexplicable

43. Spot an identical or odd couple

44. Spot an optical illusion

45. Spot a public meltdown

46. Spot an 'X' in the sky made by vapour trails

47. Spot a moment of pure slapstick

48. Spot a film set in action

49. Spot a cat with a moustache

50. See a lightning strike

51. Spot lost treasure

52. Spot someone's double

53. Spot a memorable wedding moment

54. Spot someone incognito

55. Spot something hanging on overhead wires

56. Spot a criminal act (and someone thwarting it)

57. Spot someone on their way to a fancy-dress party

58. Spot a bad tattoo

59. Spot someone go against the flow

60. Spot a lost tourist

61. See a pet that looks like its owner

62. Spot an act of road rage

63. Spot a drunken adventurer

64. Spot an invasion

65. Spot someone you know on the news

66. Spot a sporting blunder (or wonder)

67. See a multiple rainbow

68. Spot a Christmas overdose

69. Spot the next big thing

70. Spot the ultimate epic win and fail

Enter your overall scores for
each spot at the back of the book.

RULES

1. Be prepared. Always carry this book with you.

2. Be creative. Think outside the box, as some of the spots are open to interpretation.

3. Be patient. Some spotting opportunities may not present themselves to you immediately.

4. Be quick. Once you've witnessed an event, fill out the form as soon as possible, before you forget the details.

5. Pick the perfect spot to spot your spot. Some sightings can only be found in specific places.

6. You may already have spotted some of the things on the list. Chart your historic sighting until a better one comes along.

7. Share your wares. We're all in this together. Visit www.facebook.com/theMDSGbook to enter your *Modern Day Spotter* stories.

8. Add your own spots. This list of spots is far from comprehensive, so feel free to throw in your own unusual or interesting sighting.

DISCLAIMER

By purchasing or being gifted this book, you agree to the following:

The author and publisher of *The Modern Day Spotter's Guide* take no responsibility for any predicament that may befall you in your quest to witness any of the events mentioned herein.

The information that you document within the pages of this book is yours alone and in no way represents the views of the author or publisher.

The things you witness have not been spurred or instigated by the author or publisher of *The Modern Day Spotter's Guide*. It is assumed that any photographs featuring members of the public have been cleared for use by you and the subject before you upload them to any websites, including those of the publisher, author and *The Modern Day Spotter's Guide*.

Ok. Enough of this. Now go off and spot some things …

Spot something left on the roof of a car

Award points for:

5 Food and drinks

10 Items of clothing

15 Wallet, purse or keys

20 Other, e.g. documents

TASK

Find a souvenir

Find something useful that has been ejected from the roof of a passing vehicle.

Roof wreck

You'd expect to see this happen more often, and the reason you don't is probably because things left on the roof don't stay there for long. It's an easy mistake to make when, arriving back at the car with a half-eaten sandwich, a large coffee and other sundry items, you pop something on the roof for a few seconds in order to delve for your keys or load your shopping or children. It's only when you're hurtling along that you reach for your drink and, oh …

But it's one thing to forget a coffee, quite another to forget your life savings. In 2010, police in Essex began a theft inquiry after a pensioner drove off with £80,000 on the roof of his car. After years of stashing it under his bed, he had been going to take the money somewhere for safekeeping. Unsurprisingly, it was never recovered.

Car roof sales

Pretty much everything has been left on a car roof, including: jewellery, computers, phones, shoes, hats and gloves, wallets and purses, homework, gardening equipment, Christmas presents, frozen turkeys, animals, a police taser and even a three-year-old child.

CAPTURE THE MOMENT OR DRAW WHAT YOU SAW

Your eye-witness report

Fill out the form below and score points along the way.

| Location and date | | |

Who did this happen to?

○ ○ ○ ○ ○ ○

What was left on the roof of the vehicle?

Did the driver realise their error? Yes ○ No ○ Don't know ○

Did someone point out their mistake? Yes ○ No ○ Don't know ○

How long did it take for the item to fall off or get rescued?

After a short distance ○   After a long distance ○   It didn't fall off / I didn't see ○

How did you score?

Food/drink ☆5   Clothing ☆10   Wallet/keys ☆15   Other ☆20

TASK Find a souvenir   It was damaged, broken or useless. ☆25   It was intact, useful and usable! ☆50

Your notes

Log any other interesting observations below.

....

....

....

....

....

....

....

Final score

Spot an escaped animal

Award points for:

5 Escaped pet

10 Escaped farm animal

15 Escaped zoo animal

20 Other

TASK

To the rescue

Safely capture the escaped beast(s) and preferably collect a reward.

Animal antics

When there's an escaped animal on the loose, you'll often find out about it by way of a flyer posted through your door or taped to a telegraph pole, usually featuring the badly photocopied face of a cat with a name like Schrödinger looking blankly out at you. But in 2008 police in the Netherlands had to hunt down and round up a troupe of animals who'd escaped from a nearby travelling circus. The breakaway gang comprised of fifteen camels, two zebras, some llamas, a number of pigs and a very conspicuous giraffe.

Escaped animals can be seen all over the land: the south of England is a great place to spot one of many thousands of escaped exotic birds that have flocked and bred; and the UK's wild moors and valleys are the best places to glimpse elusive big cats.

Fancy-dress escape drill

Once a year, at Tokyo's Ueno Zoo, one or more zookeepers dress up in animal costumes and make a break for freedom. In 2012 staff hunted down and successfully recaptured a two-man papier mâché rhino. After the all clear, the rhino was returned to the art cupboard.

CAPTURE THE MOMENT OR DRAW WHAT YOU SAW

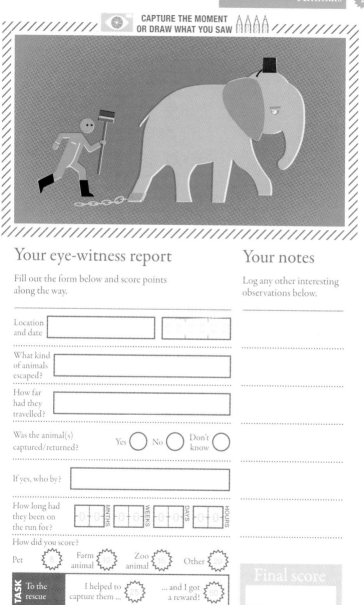

Your eye-witness report

Fill out the form below and score points along the way.

Location and date		

What kind of animals escaped?	

How far had they travelled?	

Was the animal(s) captured/returned?   Yes ◯   No ◯   Don't know ◯

If yes, who by?	

How long had they been on the run for?   0 0 MONTHS   0 0 WEEKS   0 0 DAYS   0 0 HOURS

How did you score?

Pet ⟨5⟩   Farm animal ⟨10⟩   Zoo animal ⟨15⟩   Other ⟨20⟩

TASK To the rescue   I helped to capture them ... ⟨25⟩   ... and I got a reward! ⟨50⟩

Your notes

Log any other interesting observations below.

Final score

Spot an unusual-shaped cloud

Award points for:

- **5** Animal
- **10** Object
- **15** Face or figure
- **20** Rude object

Cirrusly unusual

As clouds are constantly changing shape, it's highly probable you'll be able to see whatever you want to see, provided you're in the right place at the right time and have the necessary patience. But while you're waiting for that perfectly shaped cloud to form, here are some other sky sculptures to look out for, all of which have been previously sighted: from animals of all kinds – pigs, rabbits, bears, horses and unicorns – to famous people, such as Maggie Thatcher and Elvis Presley, along with images of Jesus on the cross, love hearts and nuclear explosions.

It would be better still to spot a natural cloud phenomenon, such as the roll, shelf or mammatus formations. Or the giant sky cock. Keep your eyes on the skies for these rare and spectacular events.

Unidentified floating objects

Lenticular clouds offer the best extra-terrestrial-like visions. These rare formations create saucer shapes in the sky which have a tendency to trigger numerous calls to the Ministry of Defence, warning against an impending alien invasion.

CAPTURE THE MOMENT OR DRAW WHAT YOU SAW

Your eye-witness report

Fill out the form below and score points along the way.

Location and date

What did you see?

Ring the words that best describe the cloud you saw.

Fluffy	White	Deformed	Awe-inspiring
Fantastical	Large	Impressionistic	Happy
Natural	Funny	Abstract	Small
Human-like	Thing	Other-worldly	Scary
Grey	Beautiful	Weird	Angular
Badly drawn	Detailed	Obscene	Cartoon-like
Angry	Ugly	Cute	Rubbish

How did you score?

Animal ⛆ 5   Object ⛆ 10   Face or figure ⛆ 15   Rude ⛆ 20

TASK Phenomenally rare   I saw a natural cloud phenomenon ... ⛆ 25   ... and here's a photo to prove it. ⛆ 50

Your notes

Log any other interesting observations below.

Final score

See the face of ___Jesus†___ in ___your soup___

Award points for:

5 Anonymous face

10 B to Z listers, e.g. reality TV stars and soap stars

15 A listers, e.g. George Clooney, Barack Obama, Michael Jackson

20 Jesus and other religious figures

TASK

Fake it

Fake a food portrait of someone famous.

Can't face it

Since the discovery of Christ's likeness upon the Shroud of Turin many centuries ago, believers and non-believers alike have been finding the face of Jesus, or something like it, in all sorts of surprising places. Food stuffs seem to be a particular favourite, with Christ appearing on a slice of burnt toast, in a half-eaten Kit Kat, within a jar of Marmite, on a fish stick, a pancake, a three-cheese pizza and a burnt frying pan, to name but a few. The Virgin Mary turned up in a similar vein on a grilled cheese sandwich. Away from the kitchen, the Son of God has also appeared on the base of an iron, in farmers' fields in Hungary (via Google Earth – see No. 31) and even on the surface of Mars. It seems that God is trying to tell us that He's always watching us. So don't do anything bad, OK? Did you check your cappuccino froth at breakfast this morning?

† It's not all about Jesus ...

Other famous faces have also made unusual cameos. For example, ET's visage was spotted in a felled tree's rings. But second to Jesus in popularity are Hitler sightings – his likeness has been found in cherry tomatoes, cats' faces (see No. 49) and a house exterior (see No. 29).

Your eye-witness report

Fill out the form below and score points along the way.

Location and date

CAPTURE THE MOMENT OR DRAW WHAT YOU SAW

What did you see?

How did you score?

Anon 〈5〉   B- to Z-lister 〈10〉   A-lister 〈15〉   A religious figure 〈20〉

TASK Fake it. My portrait fooled ...   ... a friend or family member. 〈25〉   ... a newspaper or Internet site. 〈50〉

Your notes

Log any other interesting observations below.

....

....

....

....

....

....

Final score

Spot a commuter miss ___their stop___

Award points for:

5 Missing the bus or train by seconds

10 Being delayed by someone or something

15 Being distracted or engrossed in a book, conversation or phone

20 Sleeping through their stop

TASK

Mind the gap

Give a commuter a helping hand. Hold the door, Delay the bus or wake them up just in time for their stop.

Hit and miss

The daily commute is a necessary evil of modern life for many of us, and a mis-set alarm clock or uncooperative bus driver can turn a bad journey into a bad day. Turning the corner to see that your bus has already arrived leaves you with a split-second decision: to peg it to the stop or not. Those who choose to run risk failure and humiliation. Missing the train is worse: the doors closing in your face, the hellishly long pause afterwards while a carriageful of faces stare out at you, before the train slowly pulls away. You've probably been on both sides of those doors at some time or another. And it's not just about getting on (or not). Becoming engrossed in a conversation or a book, not paying attention to announcements or falling asleep are among the many pitfalls that lie between a commuter and his or her destination.

Before you do the bus sprint, do the maths

Work out the probability of making the bus with this equation: your distance from the bus ÷ the number of people at the bus stop – the average time taken by each person to board × the lateness of the bus = a lung-busting sprint and a boarding success or failure.

CAPTURE THE MOMENT OR DRAW WHAT YOU SAW

Your eye-witness report

Fill out the form below and score points along the way.

Your notes

Log any other interesting observations below.

Location and date

Who did this happen to?

M F

Where were you?

On the vehicle ◯

At the station/stop ◯

Passing by ◯

What mode of public transport was involved?

Bus ◯ Tube train ◯ Train or tram ◯ Plane ◯ Boat or ferry ◯

How did they seem?

Unbothered ◯ Embarrassed ◯ Amused ◯ Annoyed ◯ Resigned ◯

Did they ...

... throw stuff? ◯ ... scream and shout? ◯ ... jump up and down? ◯ ... swear? ◯ All of these ◯

How did you score?

Late ✦5 Delayed ✦10 Engrossed/distracted ✦15 Asleep/drunk ✦20

TASK Mind the gap

I tried to help but they didn't make it. ✦25 They made it with my help. ✦50

Final score

Spot an amusing place name

Award points for:

 5   Unpronounceable

10   Amusing

15   Innuendo

20   Swear word

TASK

Name & shame

Ask a passerby for directions to your amusingly named location.

Rude town

The world is full of amusingly named places. You may be unfortunate enough to live in one, but if not, don't laugh at those who do. One day you might find yourself lost in Wetwang, or searching for Anus. In France, you may need to make a stop at Condom, prior to visiting Corps-Nuds, (naked bodies). The USA offers Intercourse and Climax, genteel places compared with the Austrian town pronounced 'fooking', but spelled a little differently. Still it's better than visiting Hell (Michigan, USA). The UK is the king of the innuendo: you can find a Devil's Lapful (Northumberland) and glimpse an East Breast (Inverclyde). Road names have also been known to induce a childish snigger: Grope Lane (Shropshire), Scratchy Bottom (Dorset), Menlove Avenue (Liverpool) and, the funniest one of all, Ha-Ha Road (London).

You are here

¹ **Corps-Nuds**: Brittany, France • ² **Condom**: Gers, France • ³ **Lower Dicker**: East Sussex, UK; **Happy Bottom**: Dorest, UK; **Wetwang**: East Yorkshire, UK; **Friars Entry**: Oxford, UK • ⁴ **Anus**: Burgundy, France & **Middelfart**: Denmark • ⁵ **Shitterton**: Dorset, UK • ⁶ **Ha-Ha Road**: Greenwich, London.

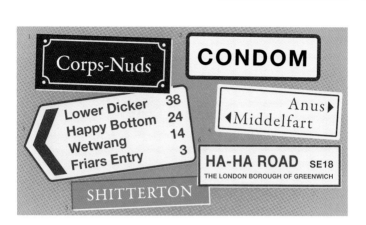

Your eye-witness report

Fill out the form below and score points along the way.

Location and date

CAPTURE THE MOMENT OR DRAW WHAT YOU SAW

How did you score?

Unpronounceable {5} Amusing {10} Innuendo {15} Swear word {20}

TASK Name and shame — I asked for directions ... {35} ... and I managed to keep a straight face. {50}

Your notes

Log any other interesting observations below.

....

....

....

....

....

....

Final score

Spot a photo bombing

Award points for:

 5 The bombing of a photo you're in

 10 Witnessing a photo bombing from afar

15 Taking a photo that got bombed

20 Being the photo bomber

TASK

You're the bomb

Execute a successful photo bomb completely unnoticed.

The recipe for the perfect photo bombing

A photo bomber can strike as if from nowhere and their target is innocent people. These audacious individuals are set on ruining a perfectly composed photo by popping into shot just as the camera clicks, and girning or pulling a face before disappearing just as stealthily. They often go unnoticed until the photos are reviewed.

Accidental photo bombings are usually the best, especially when the background bomber is captured with a surprised or deadpan stare. They frequently feature dogs, cats, birds and other passing animals. In 2009, a holiday snap of a couple posing in front of lake appeared on the Internet. Their self-timed photo was bombed by a squirrel, later dubbed 'Crasher squirrel', whose infamy created a meme of photoshopped images all bombed by the same inquisitive face.

Bomb squad

Most photo bombings are opportunistic, but just occasionally a photo bomb will be meticulously planned far in advance, such as the famous twelve-man Manchester United team photo taken before their Champions League match against Bayern Munich in 2001.

**CAPTURE THE MOMENT
OR DRAW WHAT YOU SAW**

Your eye-witness report

Fill out the form below and score points along the way.

Your notes

Log any other interesting observations below.

Location and date

Who or what was the main subject of the photo?

You | Family/friend(s) | Colleagues | Pets/animals | Strangers | Objects/scenery

Who was the photo bomber?

You | Family/friend | A colleague | Pets/animals | A stranger | A child

What expression did the bomber have?   Grin ◯   Grimace ◯   Surprise ◯   Indifference ◯

Was the photo ...   ... ruined? ◯   ... improved? ◯

How did you score?

I was in it 5   Seen from afar 10   I took it 15   I bombed it 20

TASK I bombed a photo ...   ... but I didn't get away with it. 25   ... and nobody noticed. 30

Final score

Spot a ___movie___ mistake

Award points for:

 5 Serious plot holes

 10 Continuity errors

 15 Film crew or equipment in shot

20 Other, e.g. accidents, factual or historical inaccuracies

TASK
My Mistake

Be the first to report a movie mistake online.

Scene stealer

It's easy to get lost in a great film until a glaring error jolts you right back into reality. If the website **Moviemistakes.com** is anything to go by, hardly a film has been made that didn't have an error or two in it – or, in the case of *Apocalypse Now*, 395.

The most common mistakes tend to be continuity errors. For example, props or actors might unintentionally move or change appearance between shots. Things that were broken might magically repair themselves. But also keep your eyes peeled for a crew member or piece of filming equipment in plain view (e.g. *Pirates of the Caribbean: The Curse of the Black Pearl* and *One Flew Over the Cuckoo's Nest*) technology from the future in the ancient past (e.g. *Gladiator*); and costume malfunctions (e.g. *Return of the Jedi*)

A clanger

One of the most famous movie mistakes is in *Star Wars*. It captures the moment a stormtrooper bangs his head on the door frame as he enters the control room. When the movie was re-released on DVD the appropriate sound effect was added. If you can't hide it, go with it.

Your eye-witness report

Fill out the form below and score points along the way.

Your notes

Log any other interesting observations below.

Location and date

CAPTURE THE MOMENT OR DRAW WHAT YOU SAW

Name of the movie here

How did you score?

Plot 5 Continuity 10 Equipment or crew 15 Other 20

TASK My mistake   I reported it online. 25   I was the first to report it online. 50

Final score

....

....

....

....

....

....

Spot a wild animal using public transport

Award points for:

- **5**   Vermin, e.g. rats, mice and cockroaches
- **10**   Pet adventure: e.g. stray dogs, cats and farm animals
- **15**   Urban wildlife: e.g. pigeons, foxes and squirrels
- **20**   Wild and exotic: e.g. bears, deer, snakes and lions

TASK

All aboard

See an animal hitching a ride on another animal.

A to Zoo

It's easy to complain about our public transport system, but it's a great place to observe some of the finer details of modern life, and the most ordinary journey can be spiced up by the guest appearance of some rather unusual passengers.

Pigeons are probably the easiest wild creature to spot on public transport, as not only are they used to living in our shadows, but they've got superb homing abilities – and why fly when you can ride the last few stops? You'd probably be less happy to spot a mouse or rat on an underground train, but you certainly wouldn't be the first. Squirrels have also been seen on buses, and foxes on trains. In Moscow, stray dogs have learned to use the trains to commute into town in search of food during the day, and then return home at night.

Horse Riding

You're less likely to see larger four-legged beasts on public transport, but it can happen. In 2011 a man was ejected from a train for boarding it with his horse in Wrexham, UK, while a deer was once spotted riding on top of a cargo train in Burlington, USA.

CAPTURE THE MOMENT
OR DRAW WHAT YOU SAW

Your eye-witness report

Fill out the form below and score points along the way.

Location and date

Mode of transport

Was the animal ... ... an accidental prisoner? ◯ ... a non-paying customer? ◯

Was the animal ... tame? ◯ ... nervous? ◯ ... wild? ◯

Did you see the animal get on? Yes ◯ No ◯ If yes, where?

Did you see the animal get off? Yes ◯ No ◯ If yes, where?

How did you score?

Vermin 5   Pet adventure 10   Urban wildlife 15   Wild and exotic 20

TASK
I saw an animal ... ... riding on the same species of animal. 25 ... riding on a different species. 50

Your notes

Log any other interesting observations below.

Final score

Spot a modern-day shooting star

Award points for:

5 A meteor or comet

10 A satellite or space station

15 A crashing satellite or space junk

20 A crashing meteor or asteroid

TASK

Heavens above!

Capture your shooting star on camera (e.g. see footage of the Russia meteor on Valentine's day 2013 http://goo.gl/ECtsi)

Heaven's above

In the old days, shooting stars were limited to meteors, comets and, if you were really lucky (or unlucky depending on your point of view), an asteroid. But in the last fifty years humankind has put its stamp on the heavens and now the solar system's natural shooting stars have been joined by a whole host of new heavenly bodies, such as satellites, space stations and, thanks to a few bad judgements and mistakes down here on Earth, a huge amount of assorted space junk.

Increasingly, pieces of debris from satellite collisions or defunct satellites are finding their way back to Earth in spectacular fashion. To help you rest easy, you can keep an eye on things with the help of websites like www.heavensabove.com or by downloading apps that track the flight paths of these potentially deadly objects.

Near misses. Some unwanted things from space ...

In 1979, the NASA space station Skylab fell to Earth, creating a trail of debris that hit Western Australia. In 1969, five Japanese fishermen were injured when they were hit by unknown space debris (believed to be of Russian origin).

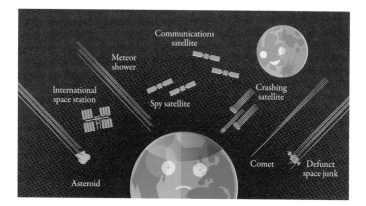

International space station

Asteroid

Meteor shower

Communications satellite

Spy satellite

Crashing satellite

Comet

Defunct space junk

Your eye-witness report

Fill out the form below and score points along the way.

Location and date

CAPTURE THE MOMENT OR DRAW WHAT YOU SAW

How did you score?

A streak of light 〜5〜 Man-made light 〜10〜 Burning debris 〜15〜 Death & destruction 〜20〜

TASK Heavens above! I captured a celestial event ... 〜25〜 ... and my footage made the news. 〜50〜

Your notes

Log any other interesting observations below.

....

....

....

....

....

....

Final score

Spot someone in a time warp

Award points for:

5 1960s–1990s

10 1920s–1950s

15 Pre-1920s

20 The future

TASK

Classic!

See a time-warped car, train or plane.

Back to the future

What goes around comes around, especially in fashion. These days there's a thriving community of vintage-lovers eager to emulate the fashion and habits of the good old days. Where once it was only the sixties, seventies and, regrettably, the eighties that seemed to make a regular fashion comeback, now it's the thirties, forties and fifties that are truly swinging. It probably won't take you long to find a prime example, but more points are on offer for spotting those genuine eccentrics who adopt styles from even earlier eras – the 'antique' years. You might be lucky enough to see an Edwardian or Victorian, or at least some twisted version of that style, like the nineteenth-century futurism of Steampunk. This is not about fancy-dress and costumes; it's about stylistic blasts from the past.

And it's not just about clothes. What you're looking for isn't simply someone wearing flares, a swing skirt or a jumpsuit, but an individual whose face looks temporally out of place too. It's about hairstyle, make-up and accessories, of course, but it's also about a certain look or type of beauty that reminds you of people in pictures, photos or films from another time. Hopefully you'll see someone who is the complete time-travelling package.

CAPTURE THE MOMENT
OR DRAW WHAT YOU SAW

POLICE PUBLIC CALL BOX

Your eye-witness report

Fill out the form below and score points
along the way.

Location
and date

Who did you see?

What were they
doing?

What era did they
appear to come from?

Which of the following
looked time-warped?

Hair   Make-up   Clothes   Face

How much did they stand out?

Not
much

A
bit

Quite
a bit

A
lot

You couldn't
miss them

How did you score?

'60s-'90s 5   '20s-'50s 10   Pre-'20s 15   The future 20

TASK Classic!

I saw a
time warped
vehicle ... 25

... with a time-
warped driver/
pilot/passenger. 50

Your notes

Log any other interesting
observations below.

Final score

Spot a living statue on a break

Award points for:

 5 Chatting to a passer-by

 10 On the phone

15 Eating or drinking

20 Going to the loo or heading home in their outfit

TASK

Stony silence

Make a living statue laugh. Just don't make him angry ...
http://goo.gl/xJnqZ

Still here

As you explore the tourist hotspots in any major city, you'll no doubt stumble across at least one statue that thinks it's a person. These street performers need to be in character the entire time they're in view of their passing audience, and this means moving as little as possible except when money has been deposited into the upturned hat.

This impressive dedication to their art makes spotting a street statue on a break the holy grail. Few have had the pleasure of seeing Michelangelo's David in the queue for a lunchtime hot dog or the Venus de Milo window shopping for a new bodywarmer. However, being a human statue must be thirsty work and unless they've had a second bladder installed, they'll have to leave their plinth sooner or later. Keep your eyes peeled for a Statue of Liberty in a queue for the loo, in the hope of a little liberation of their own.

I'm still standing

Go to Arnhem, the Netherlands, in August, and you'll be surrounded by living statues. But as competitors in the World Championship of Living Statues, the odds are you still won't catch one moving.

Your eye-witness report

Fill out the form below and score points along the way.

Your notes

Log any other interesting observations below.

Location and date

CAPTURE THE MOMENT OR DRAW WHAT YOU SAW

....

....

....

....

....

....

How did you score?

Chatting 5   On the phone 10   Eating/drinking 15   Toilet/home 20

TASK Stony silence   I made a living statue smile. 25   I made a living statue laugh. 50

Final score

Spot a wardrobe malfunction

Award points for:

 5 New dress, e.g. labels and stickers left on

10 Fancy dress, e.g. when things get attached to clothes or shoes

15 Can't dress, e.g. inside out, back to front, sock in trousers, stuck zips

20 Won't dress, e.g. when clothes reveal too much

TASK

Sort it out

Point out someone's wardrobe malfunction.

Unnecessary accessories

Fashion is a minefield for many reasons, but one of those has to be the wardrobe malfunction, in which clothes conspire to humiliate the unwary wearer. No one is immune. You simply haven't lived if you've never wandered around with a sock lump down your trouser leg.

People are often caught out by new clothes, as they seem to have an ever-increasing multitude of labels attached to them, not all of which are obvious on first inspection. Some of the size stickers they attach to trouser legs and the bottom of shoes can be particularly sly. And on the subject of new shoes, you can often tell someone who has yet to break theirs in. Also watch out for garments that are worn inside out or back to front and clothes that reveal more than they were intended to. A strapless top, for example, is always a risky fashion choice, as gravity will be working against it. And some skirts will not stay down in a wind or when you bend over.

As for toilet trips: gentlemen, remember your flies were once down and they need to be back up; while, ladies, remember that the skirt that went up has simply got to come back down. And preferably without toilet paper trailing under it.

CAPTURE THE MOMENT
OR DRAW WHAT YOU SAW

Your eye-witness report

Fill out the form below and score points
along the way.

Your notes

Log any other interesting
observations below.

Location
and date

Who did this happen to?

○ ○ ○ ○ ○ ○ ○

What item of cloth-
ing malfunctioned?

Did the
wearer
notice? Yes ○ No ○

Did they see
anyone else
notice? Yes ○ No ○

If yes, what was their reaction?

Blushing ○ Embarrass-
ment ○ Tears ○ Laughing ○

Screams ○ Hiding ○ Subtle
adjustments ○ Indiffer-
ence ○

How did you score?

New
dress 5

Fancy
dress 10

Can't
dress 15

Won't
dress 20

TASK Sort it out

They hated me
for pointing
it out. 25

They loved me
for pointing
it out. 50

Final score

Spot an invisible foe attack

Award points for:

5   Agitated and flailing arms

10   Standing up or moving away

15   Screaming and/or running

20   All of the above

TASK

Bee a hero

Capture or divert the attacking foe.

Buzz off

Picnics, pub lunches and al fresco dining with friends are among the many joys of summertime. But expect the party to be crashed by at least one unexpected aerial assailant. Like Russian roulette, it's a game of chance as to whom the kamikaze terrorist will descend upon, but once chosen, the victim will quickly become apparent.

It starts with a buzz past the ear, then the victim's defences spring into action. An early sign of attack might be distraction from conversation, quickly progressing to jumpiness and agitation. After a while, the urge to stand up becomes overpowering, coupled with an inability to operate the arms in a disciplined and graceful manner. The resulting flapping and flailing is finally synchronised with the barely controlled urge to run away. Screaming is optional.

The usual suspects

These include wasps, bees, mosquitoes and flies, but assaults often occur without the perpetrator ever being spotted by onlookers. Similar reactions may be observed in web-in-face and UFO-in-the-hair encounters.

CAPTURE THE MOMENT
OR DRAW WHAT YOU SAW

Aaaaaarrrrggggghhhh

Your eye-witness report

Fill out the form below and score points along the way.

Your notes

Log any other interesting observations below.

Location and date | 0 0 0 0 0 0

Who did this happen to?

M F ? (figures) ○ ○ ○ ○ ○ ○

Victim's name, if known

Did the victim get stung? Yes ○ No ○ Don't know ○

Was the creature provoked? Yes ○ No ○ Don't know ○

Who was the culprit? Wasp ○ Bee ○ Mosquito ○ Fly ○ Spider ○ Beetle ○ Locust ○

Moth ○ Butterfly ○ Other [ ] Don't know ○

How did you score?

Flailing arms 5 | Moving away 10 | Screaming/running 15 | All 20

TASK Bee a hero | I sent it packing. 25 | I caught it. 50

Final score

Spot someone using unusual transport

Award points for:

 5 Fantastical four-wheeler

 10 Phenomenal three-wheeler

 15 Extraordinary two-wheels

20 Weird one- or no-wheelers, e.g. a space-hopper, stilts, boat, plane or pogo stick

TASK

Pimp your ride

Customise your bike's look or functionality.

Wheely good

One wheel adequate: The unicyclist is free to do a spot of texting, map-reading or late breakfasting on the move. The same goes for the wheelbarrowist, providing they have someone to push them.

Two wheels good: There are some unusual bikes out there, from penny-farthings and tandems to customised contraptions for additional storage, speed, comfort or rain protection. For example, look out for bikes where the front wheel has been replaced by a shopping cart, for the purpose of transporting goods and children. You may also spot a motorised two-wheel mobile, such as the idiot-proof Segway.

Three wheels ample: Recumbent trikes (and bikes) are popular with cyclists keen on getting an extra half hour lie-in while their legs cycle them to work. Also look out for cute three-wheeler cars and vans.

Four wheels bad: In our drive for eco-friendly transport, cars have become the bad guys, but there are still plenty of petrol heads out there, some of whom go the extra mile and own a head-turning set of wheels, be it a classic automobile, a futuristic batmobile or a garishly spray-painted look-at-me-mobile.

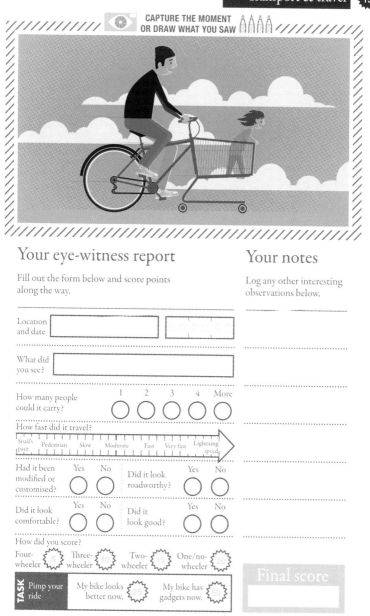

CAPTURE THE MOMENT
OR DRAW WHAT YOU SAW

Your eye-witness report

Fill out the form below and score points along the way.

Your notes

Log any other interesting observations below.

| Location and date | | |

| What did you see? | |

How many people could it carry?

1   2   3   4   More
◯ ◯ ◯ ◯ ◯

How fast did it travel?

Snail's pace   Pedestrian   Slow   Moderate   Fast   Very fast   Lightning speed

Had it been modified or customised?
Yes ◯ No ◯

Did it look roadworthy?
Yes ◯ No ◯

Did it look comfortable?
Yes ◯ No ◯

Did it look good?
Yes ◯ No ◯

How did you score?

Four-wheeler 5   Three-wheeler 10   Two-wheeler 15   One/no-wheeler 20

TASK Pimp your ride   My bike looks better now. 25   My bike has gadgets now. 50

Final score

Spot an amusing news headline

Award points for:

 Funny

 Misleading

15 Nonsensical

20 All of the above

TASK

Headline act

Become the subject of
a newspaper headline,
preferably an amusing one.

Read all about it

With a limited amount of space to grab potential readers, newspapers need to convey the key facts of a story with drama and brevity. But sometimes this economic and sensational use of language can catch the attention for all the wrong reasons. It can often lead to misinterpretation. For example, **'EMERGENCY AS PLANE HEADS TO NORWICH'** could be read as **'SCARY METAL BIRD RUN FOR YOUR LIVES'** In extreme cases, it may result in a complete lack of sense whatsoever. Take the paradoxical **'TIME CAPSULE BURIED – 10 YEARS LATE'**, for instance. Headlines are good at presenting a dull story as something else entirely, often to comic effect. When looking for the best examples, the more local the publication the better, as you may just catch sight of hard-hitting headlines like **'CAT STUCK IN TREE'** or **'LORRY MOUNTS KERB'**.

Classic Headlines

The *Sunday Sport* was famous for its absurd front page headlines. Classics include: **'STATUE OF ELVIS FOUND ON MARS'**, **'MONKEY LANDS PLANE'** and **'HIDE AND SEEK CHAMP FOUND DEAD IN CUPBOARD'**.

* A headline from the Norwich Evening News.

LOCAL NEWS

TIME CAPSULE BURIED – 10 YEARS LATE*

POLICE PUBLIC CALL BOX

Your eye-witness report

Fill out the form below and score points along the way.

Your notes

Log any other interesting observations below.

Location and date

0 0 0 0 0 0

CAPTURE THE MOMENT
OR DRAW WHAT YOU SAW

STOP PRESS
PLACE A PHOTO
OF YOUR AMUSING
NEWS HEADLINE
HERE

Which newspaper did the headline come from?

How did you score?

Funny ☆ 5 ☆ Misleading ☆ 10 ☆ Nonsensical ☆ 15 ☆ All ☆ 20 ☆

TASK Headline act | I made the news. ☆ 25 ☆ | I hit the headlines. ☆ 50 ☆

Final score

Spot a thieving seagull

Award points for:

5 Something found

10 Something stolen

15 Something inedible

20 All of the above

TASK

Feed the birds

Improve the unhealthy junk food diet of a seagull by offering it a nutritious snack.

So gull-ible

Not content with scavenging the detritus we leave behind us on the seafront, seagulls frequently terrorise picnicking pensioners and kids with ice creams. And now these large, taloned birds have spread their wings and flown inland in search of the plentiful and varied delights of takeaways and street food, homemade or gourmet. The choice is epic and, in some places, served up in one all-you-can-eat buffet, better known to us as a mountainous rubbish tip.

Summer is the best time to spot these marauding muggers, as they have young to feed and protect, and multitudes of people are lunching outside to grab some sunshine. There's no clear way to tackle them, unless you happen to have a hawk about you. But if you don't, look after your fingers, because seagulls ain't choosy.

Seagull safety tips

Put your shopping in thick bags when gulls are on the prowl; carrier bags are not beak-proof. Don't make yourself a target by eating in view of these birds, but, if you must, wear earplugs: their calls can be deafening, and a clinically timed shriek can make you drop your pasty.

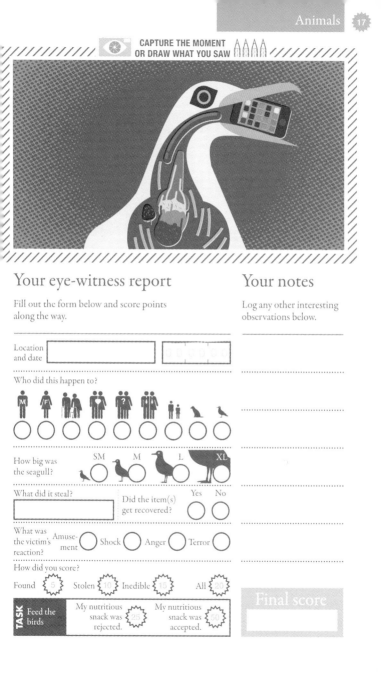

CAPTURE THE MOMENT
OR DRAW WHAT YOU SAW

Your eye-witness report

Fill out the form below and score points along the way.

Your notes

Log any other interesting observations below.

Location and date

Who did this happen to?

How big was the seagull?   SM   M   L   XL

What did it steal?   Did the item(s) get recovered?   Yes   No

What was the victim's reaction?   Amuse-ment   Shock   Anger   Terror

How did you score?

Found 5   Stolen 10   Inedible 15   All 20

TASK Feed the birds   My nutritious snack was rejected. 25   My nutritious snack was accepted. 50

Final score

Spot an embarrassed parent

Award points for:

 Meltdown mortification

 Bad behaviour shame

 Awkward question embarrassment

 Private revelation humiliation

TASK

Community care

Give someone's unruly child a good telling off.

Why, oh why ...

Children, and particularly young children who have yet to become fully socially aware, have enormous potential to embarrass their parents in public, be it with meltdowns on the scale of nuclear explosions, excruciatingly direct questions about bodily functions or people around them, or the public announcement of something said or done in private.

A tantrum can evoke a variety of emotions in an onlooker. Those who are pregnant or have kids of their own may feel sympathetic, and relieved that it's not happening to them. For those without kids, it can inspire fear and terror, or the urge to quash the nasty noise-making beast. In a meltdown situation, no help can be offered, no eye contact should be made, just pretend nothing is happening and move along.

Other embarrassing situations for a parent include: bad behaviour, especially when a child decides to clobber another child; leaving a shop to find extra items in the buggy that weren't paid for; kids running in one direction and not coming back; and children who decide they'd rather not wear clothes. The only consolation for these parents is the prospect of many years of sweet retribution that lie ahead.

CAPTURE THE MOMENT
OR DRAW WHAT YOU SAW

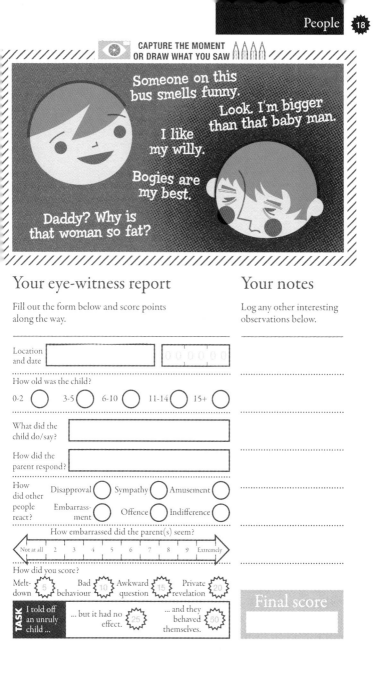

Your eye-witness report

Fill out the form below and score points along the way.

Location and date

0 0 0 0 0 0

How old was the child?

0-2 ◯   3-5 ◯   6-10 ◯   11-14 ◯   15+ ◯

What did the child do/say?

How did the parent respond?

How did other people react?

Disapproval ◯   Sympathy ◯   Amusement ◯

Embarrassment ◯   Offence ◯   Indifference ◯

How embarrassed did the parent(s) seem?

Not at all ◀ 2 3 4 5 6 7 8 9 ▶ Extremely

How did you score?

Meltdown 5   Bad behaviour 10   Awkward question 15   Private revelation 20

TASK I told off an unruly child ...   ... but it had no effect. 25   ... and they behaved themselves. 50

Your notes

Log any other interesting observations below.

Final score

See your name   *on a gravestone*

Award points for:

5 The name of someone you know on a sign, e.g. building, business or road name

10 The name of someone you know (living) on a gravestone

15 Your name on a sign

20 Your name on a gravestone

TASK

Don't I know you?

Meet someone with your name.

Death defying

Death comes to everyone in the end, but for many of us we've already been there and got the gravestone. If your name isn't too out of the ordinary, there's a good chance that somewhere in the world there's someone with the same name as you who has ceased to be ... you.

Due to a rise in the popularity of genealogy, more burial records have been released to the public, and with a little searching you may well be able to find someone who shared your name, locate their burial site and ultimately, like Scrooge, come face to face with your own inescapable fate. If you have a very common name, and you enjoy strolling in cemeteries, you may just chance across it by accident. But if you're not comfortable with graveyards, there are other places that might share all or part of your name, such as buildings, roads and businesses.

In memory of Richard Horne (1917 & 1920)

The website www.deceasedonline.com is a central database for UK burials and cremations. There are two Richard Hornes listed as being buried in the UK, one in St Pancras Cemetery (Camden), the other in Hampstead Cemetery (Camden). This entry is dedicated to them.

HERE LIES

Your eye-witness report

Fill out the form below and score points along the way.

IN LOVING MEMORY OF

First name   Middle name: (optional)   Surname

Location and date

If your name wasn't on a gravestone, what was it on?

SEIZE THE MOMENT OR DRAW WHAT YOU SAW

How did you score?

Another name: sign — 5   Another name: grave — 10   Your name: sign — 15   Your name: grave — 20

TASK I met someone with my name ...   ... and they were nothing like me. — 25   ... and we had a lot in common. — 50

Your notes

Log any other interesting observations below.

....

....

....

....

....

Final score

Spot a dancing plastic bag

Award points for:

 5 Dancing leaves

 10 Dancing papers and wrappers

 15 A dancing plastic bag

 20 All of the above

TASK

Let's dance

Film the rubbish dancers.

Blowing in the wind

The wind may be a damn nuisance at times (see No. 37), but it can also be great to watch. Paired with a playful gust, the most unlikely performers can suddenly leap into life with some enchanting results.

Take the humble plastic bag. Immortalised for ever in that scene from *American Beauty*, this environmental pest and symbol of our modern consumerist society can become a thing of beauty in the hands of the wind. So next time you see one lying in the road, slumped against the kerb like a bedraggled tramp, wait to see if a breeze picks it up and transforms it into an elegant synthetic ballerina, taking it from down and out to up and down and round and round in a matter of gusts. And the plastic bag is seldom seen dancing solo. Look out for a corps de ballet of newspapers, crisp packets, sweet wrappers and nature's own gilded dancers, the fallen leaves.

Bag it and bin it

Having captured the jiving junk and pirouetting trash on camera, wait for the wind to die down, applaud the litter loudly, then lift it into your arms and moonwalk it over to the bin.

CAPTURE THE MOMENT
OR DRAW WHAT YOU SAW

HAVE A NICE DAY

Your eye-witness report

Fill out the form below and score points along the way.

Location and date

Which words best describe what you saw?

Balletic	Beautiful	Energetic	Wistful
Lyrical	Passionate	Moody	Humorous
Playful	Boring	Exciting	Rubbish
Swooping	Darting	Diving	Spinning

How strong was the wind?

Gentle 2 3 4 5 6 7 Gale force

Did the bag attack anyone? Yes No

Did you tidy away the dancer(s)? Yes No

How did you score?

Leaves 5   Papers/wrappers 10   Plastic bag 15   All 20

TASK Let's dance   I filmed it. It was rubbish. 25   I filmed it and it was the most beautiful thing I've ever seen. 50

Your notes

Log any other interesting observations below.

Final score

Spot an awkward date

Award points for:

 5 Awkward silences

 10 Arguments and tears

 15 A rejected kiss

 20 Stood up / broke up

TASK

The drinks are on me

Order strong drinks and send them anonymously over to the couple on an awkward date.

A date with destiny

Ill-chosen words, long silences, fumbled passes, insults, arguments, even a slap or a glass of water thrown in the face ... some dates are grim to be on and excruciating to witness. And they don't come much more awkward than first ones, especially blind dates and set-ups. With heightened expectations and a desperate desire to impress (or escape), these first meetings can be fraught with awkwardness and potential disaster. And that's assuming both parties show up.

But it's not just about first dates. Those who are used to sitting in comfortable silence at home may find themselves sitting in an uncomfortable silence in public. Other long-term couples might discover that lavishing too much attention on their relationship leads to the airing and sharing of grievances, particularly once a bit of alcohol has loosened the tongue. And look out for 'date-night' couples who have escaped their young kids only to sit and yawn at each other for an hour before deciding that having fun is just too tiring.

Basically, any great night out can be sabotaged by the pressure to have a good time and draw the night to a romantic conclusion – which might make Valentine's Day an especially good time to go spotting.

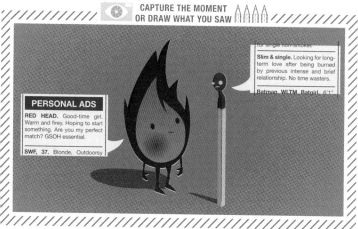

CAPTURE THE MOMENT
OR DRAW WHAT YOU SAW

Your eye-witness report

Fill out the form below and score points along the way.

Your notes

Log any other interesting observations below.

....

Location and date

....

Who was on the date?

Which words best describe what you saw?

....

Romance	Boredom	Awkwardness	Pleading
Silence	Laughter	Shouting	Crying
Cold shoulder	Resignation	Love	Embarrassment
Exhaustion	Bickering	Sharp exit	Threats
Painful	Rudeness	Remorse	Shamelessness

....

How did it end?   Happily   Angrily   Sadly   Amicably   Abruptly   Didn't see

....

How did you score?

Awkward silences **5**   Arguments **10**   Rejected kiss **15**   Break up/ stood up **20**

TASK I ordered them drinks ... ... but it only led to a fight. **25** ... and their date improved. **30**

Final score

Spot an amusingly shaped vegetable

Award points for:

5 Abnormal size

10 A face

15 Private parts

20 All of the above

TASK

Good show

Enter your homegrown oddity into a fruit or vegetable competition.

Pea cock

Amusingly shaped vegetables are something of a rarity these days, as only the best-looking produce is deemed good enough for the uniform and well-groomed shelves of the supermarket.

Abnormal fruit and vegetables are generally the result of damage during growth, often caused by wind, rain, frost and drought. A damaged vegetable will keep growing but not necessarily as nature intended. They can develop extra bits and bobs (and sometimes boobs). Sometimes fruit and vegetables are encouraged to grow into amusing or functional shapes and sizes, by restricting their growth area. If you're on the lookout for anything even slightly amusing then the best way is to grow or pick your own. With homegrown produce, you'll see there's no such thing as 'normal', particularly if you're not a gardening expert. But you'll love your veggies no matter how deformed they are, because you grew them.

Alternatively you could head down to the local farm or farmers' market to uncover the mud-covered freaks of the vegetable world. Among the undernourished and the malformed, you may even find yourself a real life Mr Potato Head, Mr Potato Legs or Mr Potato Private Parts.

Your eye-witness report

Fill out the form below and score points along the way.

Location and date [   ] [0 0 0 0 0]

*CAPTURE THE MOMENT
OR DRAW WHAT YOU SAW*

How did you score?

Abnormal {5}   A face {10}   Private parts {15}   All {20}

TASK Good show

I entered it into a competition ... {25}   ... and it won a prize! {50}

Your notes

Log any other interesting observations below.

....

....

....

....

....

....

Final score

[   ]

Spot an amusing auto-correction

Award points for:

 Gobbledegook

 Surreal nonsense

 Innuendo ladened

 Embarrassingly rude

TASK

Damn you

Get an autocorrect featured on www.damn youautocorrect.com

Word perfect

In the days before mobile phones, good writing skills were essential, but our high-speed modern-day living doesn't allow for such frivolous tasks as looking up words in a dictionary. Seconds are in short supply and checking your spelling or typing out impressive long words take up too many of them. First of all, we began to shortn wrds, so we cld say mor in a msg, and then as phones got smarter we developed new ways to reduce our message-writing time.

What we really wanted was a mind-reading tool to magically produce the exact message we wanted to write; what we got was predictive text and auto-correction, tools that masquerade as labour-saving aids, but in reality necessitate the laborious rewriting or editing of messages that have been rendered incomprehensible. In other words, that supposedly 'smart' phone in your pocket can make you look anything but. Through the mis-corrected substitution of words, messages can become at best a bit LOL, at worst complete WTF, and occasionally rather OMG, as words like 'books' become 'boobs', 'stop' becomes 'strip' and 'sew' becomes 'sex'. On the other hand, mundane conversations can turn into intriguing surreal fantasies and simple statements into dubious propositions. It's not clever, but it is funny.

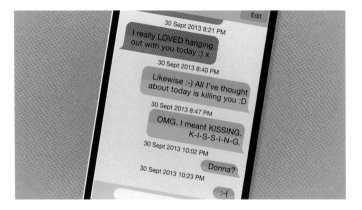

30 Sept 2013 8:21 PM
I really LOVED hanging out with you today :) x

30 Sept 2013 8:40 PM
Likewise :-) All I've thought about today is killing you :D

30 Sept 2013 8:47 PM
OMG. I meant KISSING. K-I-S-S-I-N-G.

30 Sept 2013 10:02 PM
Donna?

30 Sept 2013 10:23 PM
:-(

Your eye-witness report

Fill out the form below and score points along the way.

Your notes

Log any other interesting observations below.

Location and date

Who sent and who received the error? Tick and specify ...

YOU ○   ○ YOU

○   ○

○   ○

○   ○

Name of texters [   ] & [   ]

How did you score?

Gobble-degook **5**   Surreal message **10**   Innuendo-laden **15**   Rude **20**

TASK Damn you   My text got featured. **25**   My text was featured in the 'best of' section. **50**

Final score

Spot something unusual on a bus shelter

Award points for:

 Creative advertising

 Any unusual items, e.g. bowls of cereal, ironing boards, deck chairs

 Landscaped garden

 Guerilla art

TASK

Art attack

Create your own public art worthy of a bus stop top.

Bus tops

Gone are the days when bus shelters were merely a place for keeping people dry from the rain. Their roofs, once littered with discarded chip wrappers and half-eaten kebabs, are now being employed by wannabe Banksys as pop-up art galleries or curio havens. It's the perfect free art space, attracting passing captive top-deck audiences by the busload.

Bus stops around the globe have undergone various transformations. In the UK, there's been ornamental gardens, complete with ducks (Midsomer Norton, Somerset), and miniaturised houses with picket fences (Manchester). The vegetation exhibited on shelters along London's 55 bus route has a distinctive artistic twist, with an assortment of 'spudniks': large potatoes, sometimes painted, with cotton buds, matchsticks, pencils, pasta and similar spiky objects sticking out of them. No Nose, the street artist who created them, remains a bit of a mystery. Advertisers, too, have been responsible for some quirky bus-stop installations: in Denmark, Ikea fitted out a stop to resemble a living room; in Brazil, stops were refitted as goals; and in Vancouver the security firm 3M placed three million dollars behind unbreakable glass. If you managed to break it, the money was yours, although you were advised to read the small print first.*

---

* In actual fact, the majority of the money was fake, except for the $500 notes on the top of the pile. And you were only allowed to use your feet in an attempt to break it.

CAPTURE THE MOMENT
OR DRAW WHAT YOU SAW

dur dur   dur dur
dur dur

You're going to need a Bigger bus

Your eye-witness report

Fill out the form below and score points along the way.

Location and date			0 0 0 0 1

What did you see?

Which words best describe what you saw?

Weird	Funny	Artistic	Surreal
Fantastical	Other worldly	Great	Awful
Considered	Dumped	Thrown together	Accidental
Edible	Creepy	Natural	Unnatural
Perishable	Beautiful	Ugly	Of its time

Have you seen others like it?	Yes No	Would you consider it art?	Yes No

How did you score?

Advertising	5	Unusual items	10	Garden	15	Guerilla art	20

TASK Art attack | It's worthy of a bus shelter top. | 25 | It's worthy of an art gallery. | 50 |

Your notes

Log any other interesting observations below.

Final score

Spot a public typo

Award points for:

 5 Marketing material, e.g. shop signs, menus, adverts

 10 Book, newspaper and magazine typos

 15 Official signs and notices, e.g. on roads, in schools and museums

 20 Rude word typos, e.g. 'pubic' for 'public', 'shit' for 'shirt'

TASK

Get it right

Get a public typo corrected.

Selling mistake

Even though we all make mistakes when we're typing, there's something very satisfying about spotting other people's, particularly when the text concerned is for public consumption. It makes us feel clever for being able to read, and we wonder how it is possible for such a glaring error to have been missed by the person who wrote, edited or transcribed the text.

An exxtra letter here, a mssing one there, a couple of letters in the worng place or a bad translation and you've got yourself the necessary elements for a typo shaming. You can spot them on pub chalkboards, in menus, newspapers, leaflets and flyers, placards and even street signs and tattoos (see No. 58) ... Basically, look for typos wherever words are used. And, yes, that means this book too.

The most expensive typo in history

A costly error was caused by a typo discovered within the programming of the Mariner 1 spacecraft after it was launched in July 1962. The mission was forcefully aborted. The offending mistake, supposedly a misplaced hyphen, is judged to have cost 80 million dollars.

Your eye-witness report

Fill out the form below and score points along the way.

Location and date

CAPTURE THE MOMENT
OR DRAW WHAT YOU SAW

How did you score?

Marketing material 〈5〉 Book/newspaper 〈10〉 Notice/sign 〈15〉 Rude word 〈20〉

TASK Get it right I pointed out the mistake ... 〈25〉 ... and they corrected it. 〈50〉

Your notes

Log any other interesting observations below.

....

....

....

....

....

....

Final score

Spot a food malfunction

Award points for:

- **5** Small localised spillage

- **10** Generous coverage

- **15** Tsunami, including engulfed technology and/or bystanders

- **20** Epic, e.g. an overturned lorry food spill

TASK

In your face

Witness a food fight.

Food fight

Learning to eat is one of the first independent skills we learn, and yet it's amazing how often you see adults making as much of a mess of it as babies. From tipping your glass to your lips a fraction too early, to putting just slightly more food into your mouth than it can hold, everyone has had some experience of a food fightback.

Revenge is a dish best served hot, and a tea or coffee upset can cause quite a stir, inflicting pain and embarrassment on the victim, not to mention costly damage to nearby electronic equipment. But while knocks, trips and spills are common enough, it's not always about human incompetence. Some foods are just damn difficult to eat and would rather be worn, such as fast-melting ice creams and over-filled sandwiches, burgers or hotdogs, whose contents make a last-ditched bid for freedom as the consumer takes a bite. Other dangers lie in shaken-up drinks cans, soup slops, spaghetti splashes, jelly slips, pea escapes and shellfish wrestling. Food that is too spicy, too cold or too hot may also make a vengeful comeback and the tomato ketchup overflow has become such a classic malfunction that some people reject the ease of a squeeze in favour of the thrilling glass-bottle gamble.

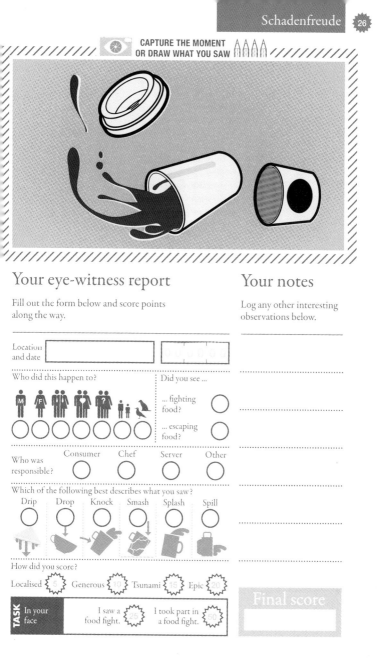

CAPTURE THE MOMENT OR DRAW WHAT YOU SAW

Your eye-witness report

Fill out the form below and score points along the way.

Your notes

Log any other interesting observations below.

Location and date

Who did this happen to?

Did you see ...

... fighting food? ◯

... escaping food? ◯

Who was responsible?

Consumer	Chef	Server	Other
◯	◯	◯	◯

Which of the following best describes what you saw?

Drip	Drop	Knock	Smash	Splash	Spill
◯	◯	◯	◯	◯	◯

How did you score?

Localised 5   Generous 10   Tsunami 15   Epic 20

TASK In your face

I saw a food fight. 15

I took part in a food fight. 30

Final score

Spot interesting facial hair

Award points for:

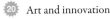

5 Size isn't everything

10 Size is everything

15 Time-warped whiskers

20 Art and innovation

TASK

Facial fashionistas

Wear some interesting facial hair or make-up.

Stash

Groucho and Karl Marx, Hitler and Charlie Chaplin, Dali and Einstein, Mario and Wario, Chewbacca and Gandalf ... They all have that one distinguishing feature in common – unforgettable facial hair.

It is easy to lose count of the number of times facial hair has been in and out of fashion. Popular in the middle ages, beards were out by the fifteenth century, back in during the sixteenth and out again in the seventeenth. They remained out until around 1850, when there was suddenly a facial hair frenzy which lasted into the 1920s. Since then we have witnessed everything from goatees, soul patches, chinstraps and neckbeards, to walruses, handlebars, mutton-chops and five o'clock shadows. Facial hair has become a free accessory and a integral way of expressing one's individuality. And some people are definitely more individual than others.

The best month to spot an interesting moustache is ...

... Movember. During the month formerly known as November, normally clean-shaven Mo Bros set out to sprout the most spectacular moustaches in order to raise money for prostate cancer charities.

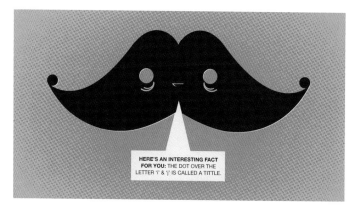

HERE'S AN INTERESTING FACT FOR YOU: THE DOT OVER THE LETTER 'i' & 'j' IS CALLED A TITTLE.

Your eye-witness report

Fill out the form below and score points along the way.

Your notes

Log any other interesting observations below.

Location and date

CAPTURE THE MOMENT OR DRAW WHAT YOU SAW

How did you score?

Minimal 5 Maximal 10 Time-warped 15 Artistic 20

TASK Facial fashionistas

I wore some interesting facial fashion ... 25 ... and now everyone's copying me. 50

Final score

Spot a celebrity lookalike

Award points for:

 5 Barely-lookalike

 10 Look-sort-of-alike

 15 Look-a-lot-alike

20 Spitting image or so bad they're actually good

TASK

Autograph hunt

Persuade the lookalike to give you their autograph.

15 seconds of fame

Celebrity spotting can be just as fun when the person you've spotted isn't really a celebrity at all. There'll be a special frisson about seeing someone famous in an everyday place doing an everyday job. You could be driven to work by a bus driver with a resemblance to Barack Obama, served your coffee by a poor man's Simon Cowell or get a parking ticket from a drab Lady Gaga. In fact these spots are worth more than professional lookalikes, who are usually a disappointment. And A- or Z-lister, it doesn't matter. Though bear in mind that with a Z-lister, you may actually be seeing the celebrity and not a lookalike.

The celebrity doesn't have to be a real person either, so long as the lookalike is. They can be a fictional person, the subject of a painting or even a cartoon character. Nor do they have to be alive. After all, people seem to spot Elvis all the time.

Loser-alike

Charlie Chaplin entered a Chaplin lookalike contest and lost so badly that he didn't even make it into the final rounds. Dolly Parton entered a Dolly lookalike contest and came second; the winner was a man.

CAPTURE THE MOMENT
OR DRAW WHAT YOU SAW

WILL
★★☆☆☆

Your eye-witness report

Fill out the form below and score points along the way.

Location and date		

Who did the celebrity lookalike resemble?	

What were they doing when you spotted them?	

Compare-alike

Place a photo of the

Place an image of the

lookalike here

actual celebrity here

How did you score?

Barely 5   Sort of 10   A lot 15   Spitting image/so bad they're good 20

TASK Autograph hunt   I got their autograph ... 25   ... and it turned out they really were a celebrity. 50

Your notes

Log any other interesting observations below.

Final score

See a face in an everyday place

Award points for:

5 Two facial features,
e.g. eyes and mouth

10 Three facial features,
e.g. eyes, nose and mouth

15 Four facial features,
e.g. eyes, nose, mouth and ears

20 Face plus body parts

TASK

Face in cyberspace

Get a photo of the face you find
featured on www.facesinplaces.
blogspot.co.uk or, even better,
in the *Faces in Places* book.

Eye spy

Some walls have ears; others have eyes. All that's needed is two adjacent pictures or wall lights. A piece of furniture sitting between them might suggest a mouth too. Viewed from the right angle, almost anything, in fact, can have a face, from cheese graters to light switches, from sinks to cupboards, from a slice of banana to a bowl of soup (see No. 4).

Once you've noticed that an inanimate object is watching you, you'll begin to see eyes everywhere you look – in screws, holes, buttons, dials, alcoves, patterns in wallpaper and wood, to name but a few. A pair of these, partnered with a well-placed tap, handle, shelf, door, zip, gap, vent, hook or anything else a bit nosey or mouthy, will result in you spotting faces in all sorts of new places.

If you need to escape the prying eyes, going outdoors may not provide the respite you crave: houses can stare out at you, trees with perfectly placed knotty eyes and hollowed gaping mouths can follow your every move, even vehicles, with their headlights, badges, grills and number plates, have faces. You might also glimpse a profile in the melting snow or long shadows of a sunny evening. Spot them before they spot you.

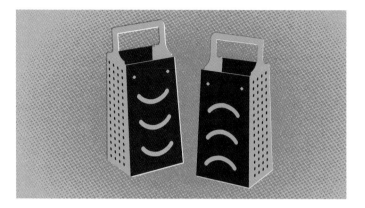

Your eye-witness report

Fill out the form below and score points along the way.

Your notes

Log any other interesting observations below.

Location and date [   ] [0 0 0 0 0 0]

👁 **CAPTURE THE MOMENT OR DRAW WHAT YOU SAW** 🖍🖍🖍🖍

....

....

....

....

....

....

How did you score?

Two features ✦5✦   Three features ✦10✦   Four features ✦15✦   Face and body parts ✦20✦

TASK Face in cyberspace | My face was featured on the site ... ✦25✦ | ... and in the book. ✦50✦

Final score
[   ]

Spot a competitive parent

Award points for:

 Boasting and one-upmanship

 Competitiveness

 Cheating in order to win

 All of the above

TASK

Beat them!

No one likes a show off, so find an opportunity to put them in their place.

Mum and dad know best

Wander down to your local park and see if you can spot a competitive dad dazzling an awestruck audience of kids with his superior football skills. All the youngsters can do is watch the white haze that was once their ball pass by them as Dad shows off with his twists and turns. Other prime locations to spot competitive fathers are school sports days and children's parties, where the competition may be against other dads as well their kids. But life is full of opportunities for competitive fathers to teach their children the valuable lesson of losing gracefully, be it playing board games at Christmas, in a race to the car, throwing stuff or knowing stuff ... Wherever something can be won, it will be won, but not by the children.

Competitiveness in mums more often takes place between mums, and may come in the form of an announcement disguised as an aside or even a complaint about how annoying/stressful/strange (but actually wonderful) it is to have such a talented son or daughter. Anything and everything can and is being achieved by a competitive mum's child: speaking fluent Spanish by the age of six, reading Tolkien by the age of three, and saying their first word inside the womb.

CAPTURE THE MOMENT OR DRAW WHAT YOU SAW

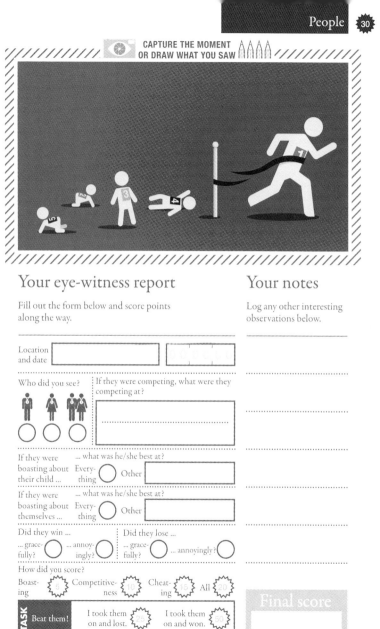

Your eye-witness report

Fill out the form below and score points along the way.

Location and date		

Who did you see? ○ ○ ○

If they were competing, what were they competing at?

If they were boasting about their child ... Every-thing ○ Other | ... what was he/she best at?

If they were boasting about themselves ... Every-thing ○ Other | ... what was he/she best at?

Did they win ...
... grace-fully? ○   ... annoy-ingly? ○

Did they lose ...
... grace-fully? ○   ... annoyingly? ○

How did you score?

Boast-ing ☆5 Competitive-ness ☆10 Cheat-ing ☆15 All ☆20

TASK Beat them! I took them on and lost. ☆25 I took them on and won. ☆50

Your notes

Log any other interesting observations below.

Final score

Spot something unusual on Google Street View

Award points for:

 See an amusing visual effect

 See an unusual event

 See someone you know

 See yourself

TASK

Spot to spot

Find one of the spots from this book in Google Street View.

Street view

When Google Street View was launched in the spring of 2007, it didn't take long for eagle-eyed users to start spotting some images to shock, amuse and intrigue. As the odd Street View cars passed by, not only did they capture the bemused looks on the faces of millions of bystanders (later pixilated), they also caught a snapshot of everyday life across the world, including all its not-so-everyday bits. Some of the more exotic scenes that can still be viewed include nudity, drunkenness, fire, traffic accidents, mooning and flashing, not to mention illegal hand-gun deals, an escaped tiger, burglaries, fights, aliens, scavenging horses, hidden messages in fields, hidden expletives and giant phalluses.

In some cases, it wasn't the subject of the image that was strange, it was the image itself. To make the camera view continuous and consistent as you scroll, the millions of photographs are stitched together, creating all sorts of bizarre effects and monstrosities along the way. Some people appear to have two heads while others have had their heads completely removed. Other anomalies include duplications, bendy aeroplanes and roads driving off into what looks like the ends of the earth, Google's Earth.

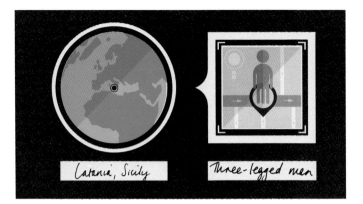

Catania, Sicily

Three-legged men

Your eye-witness report

Fill out the form below and score points along the way.

Location and date

⊙ **CAPTURE THE MOMENT OR DRAW WHAT YOU SAW**

How did you score?

Funny effect ☆ 5 Unusual event ☆ 10 Someone I know ☆ 15 Myself ☆ 20

TASK Spot to spot I saw a 5/10 point spot. ☆ 25 I saw a 15/20 point spot. ☆ 50

Your notes

Log any other interesting observations below.

....

....

....

....

....

....

Final score

Spot a bird-poo victim

Award points for:

5 Long shot (within a metre)

10 Near miss (within a few centimetres)

15 Glancing blow to the body

20 Direct hit to the head

TASK

Duck!

Save a bird-poo victim.

Totally pooped

Birds have lived on this planet for millions of years longer than us, so when we appeared and set about destroying their natural habitats, swapping their beautiful woodlands for our artificially constructed human roosts, it's no surprise they used them as vantage points from which to launch their perfectly timed semi-liquid revenge.

While city dwellers dread the pooping pigeon, those on the coast fear the flight path of the seagull – a bird that can carpet-bomb on the wing at will. You'll probably spot your victim strolling along the seafront, sitting on the steps below a statue in a public square or under the trees in a park. And it's not only birds that vent their frustration at us with fecal strikes. Primates in zoos have been known to conduct dirty protests by throwing their droppings at gawping visitors.

A hail of bad reviews

In 2010 the rock band Kings of Leon were pooed offstage in the Verizon Amphitheatre, St Louis, by a flock of pigeons that stormed the gig and perched directly above them. The gig was quickly abandoned as the onslaught from their airborne critics became too much to bear.

CAPTURE THE MOMENT
OR DRAW WHAT YOU SAW

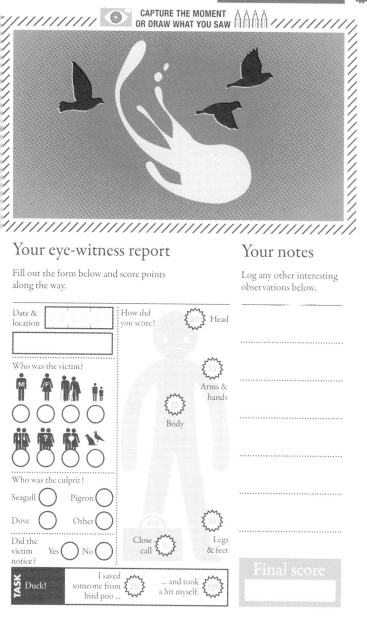

Your eye-witness report

Fill out the form below and score points along the way.

| Date & location | | How did you score? | 20 Head |

Who was the victim?

M   F   👥   👦

Who was the culprit?

Seagull ◯   Pigeon ◯

Dove ◯   Other ◯

Did the victim notice?   Yes ◯   No ◯

TASK Duck!   I saved someone from bird poo ... 25   ... and took a hit myself. 50

10 Arms & hands

15 Body

Close call 5   Legs & feet 10

Your notes

Log any other interesting observations below.

....

....

....

....

....

....

Final score

Spot a dropped photo

Award points for:

5 A passport photo

10 A family photo

15 A funny photo

20 A risqué photo

TASK

See the world

Put a photo of yourself in a bottle with your email address on the back and send it out into the world.

Snapped up

Finding a photo is like glimpsing through a window into a stranger's life. Who are they? Where is that? How did the photo end up here? Why has someone been ripped out of the picture? You begin to build a story around the characters, using the photo as a clue.

It's true that in this digital age it's becoming less common to find lost photos dropped in the street, but it's not impossible if you keep a sharp look-out. Passport photos are your best bet. They're vital when travelling and small, so easily lost. But people might also lose photos from purses and wallets. You'll probably feel a bit like an intruder, looking at these pictures which were not meant for your eyes, and you might wander around for days expecting to see a face that matches your picture. Imagine what you would do if you did ...

One place you can definitely find a dropped photo ...

In 1972 Charles Duke, Apollo 16 astronaut, became the tenth man to walk on the moon. Before he headed back to Earth, he left behind a colour photo of himself as a boy with his family. His family snap is still there, waiting to be picked up.

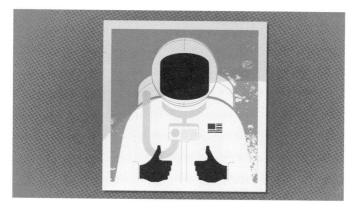

Your eye-witness report

Fill out the form below and score points along the way.

Location and date		

CAPTURE THE MOMENT
OR DRAW WHAT YOU SAW

How did you score?

Passport 5   Family 10   Funny 15   Risqué 20

TASK See the world

I never heard of my photo again. 25   My photo eventually got back to me. 50

Your notes

Log any other interesting observations below.

....

....

....

....

....

....

Final score

Spot someone with techno rage

Award points for:

 5 Audio content mild

10 Audio content obscene

15 Physical display, including bashing, kicking or throwing

20 All of the above

TASK

Control key

Invent a technique to calm yourself when techno-enraged.

Anger mismanagement

Modern technology has evolved to make our lives easier. We're enjoying an age of smart phones, keyless cars, cashless transactions, ticketless trains and tablet computers – at least we're enjoying it some of the time. For with this techno-tide comes a new kind of techno-tyranny. It can't be stopped and it's too late to turn back the clocks, except when your laptop reverts to its default date of 1 January 2008. All too often these devices turn on us, refusing to do what we need them to do, leaving us in a spluttering techno-rage in this supposed-to-be-helpful techno-age. When hourglass syndrome sets in, or the beach ball of doom makes yet another unwelcome appearance, we are pitched into a frenzy of swearing and keyboard bashing.

If you spot a techno tirade, nod sympathetically and breathe an inward sigh of relief. It wasn't your turn this time, but it soon will be.

Death by stereo: a techno love/hate playlist

Know Your Enemy – Rage Against the Machine • Kraftwerk – Computer Love • Kill Your Television – Neds Atomic Dustbin • Daft Punk – Digital Love • Paranoid Android – Radiohead

CAPTURE THE MOMENT
OR DRAW WHAT YOU SAW

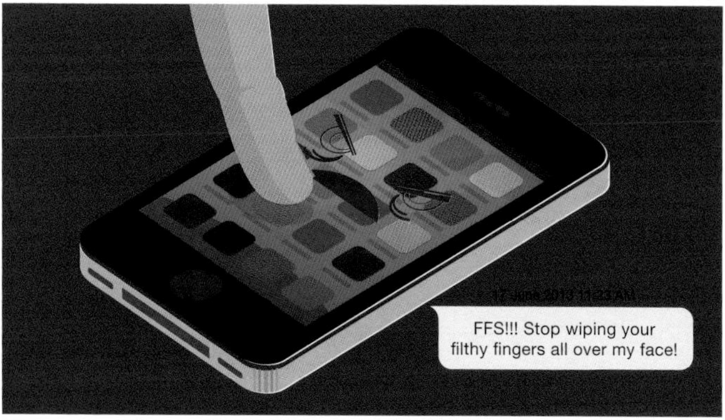

FFS!!! Stop wiping your
filthy fingers all over my face!

Your eye-witness report

Fill out the form below and score points
along the way.

Your notes

Log any other interesting
observations below.

Location
and date

Who did this happen to?

○ ○ ○ ○ ○ ○ ○ ○ ○

What were
they raging
at?

Computer Phone Cash machine Car Gaming Other tech

○ ○ ○ ○ ○ ○

What
did you
see?

Throwing Swearing Bashing Anger Breaking Thumping

○ ○ ○ ○ ○ ○

Did they make
the problem
worse?

Yes No

○ ○

Did the problem
eventually get
fixed?

Yes No

○ ○

How did you score?

Mild 5   Obscene 10   Physical 15   All 20

TASK Control key

My technique
worked. I
calmed down ... 25

... and I got my
technology
working again. 50

Final score

Spot an inappropriate T-shirt

Award points for:

5 Crude

10 Shocking

15 Offensive

20 All of the above

TASK

Loud clothing

Write a T-shirt slogan that best represents you.

T-shites

It's commonly accepted that what we wear is an expression of who we are, or who we want others to think we are. So if we wear a T-shirt displaying a design or slogan, it's a pretty good indicator of the sort of stuff we're into – from music, film and literature, to fashion, art, politics, sport, humour and even sexual preference. All these things may be a matter of taste, but most people can agree roughly where the boundaries of taste lie.

For some a T-shirt is an opportunity to show the world how hilarious, outrageous or opinionated the wearer is. There are many inappropriate T-shirts out there, some more offensive than others. They're easy to find on the internet, but less commonly seen in real-life, because most people wouldn't be seen dead in them.

The sort of T-shirts you're looking out for may allude to sexual prowess, attractiveness, certain parts of the anatomy, weight, fitness, age, intelligence and, at the extreme end, violence and prejudice. Look out for babygrows or kids' T-shirts that put words into the mouths of the children. None of these slogans need to be spelled out here, but you'll definitely know them when you see them.

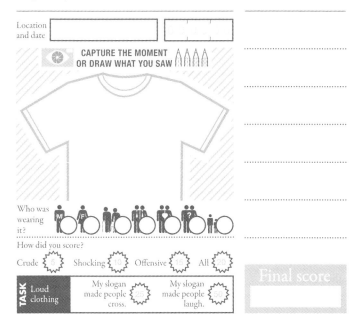

I AM THE KING OF
CENSORED

Your eye-witness report

Fill out the form below and score points along the way.

Your notes

Log any other interesting observations below.

Location and date

CAPTURE THE MOMENT
OR DRAW WHAT YOU SAW

Who was wearing it?

How did you score?

Crude 5 · Shocking 10 · Offensive 15 · All 20

TASK Loud clothing

My slogan made people cross. 25

My slogan made people laugh. 50

Final score

Spot a pigeon with ___one foot___

Award points for:

- **5** One and a half feet

- **10** One foot

- **15** Half a foot

- **20** No feet

TASK

Catch the pigeon

Get a photograph with you and the pigeon in question. Bonus points for a pigeon perching on you.

Pigeon spy

Pigeons are one of the most prolific creatures on the planet and with around 400 million of these birds worldwide (that's one pigeon for every 17 people), they shouldn't be hard to spot. Visit any city in the world and you will no doubt chance across a pigeon or two, although whether or not they have two feet remains to be seen.

Bumblefoot (or 'popcorn foot') is a condition that affects birds and rodents. The infection can create an unsightly abscess and cause distortion in the feet, which sometimes results in the loss of a foot altogether. This is a real shame for pigeons as it only makes these birds (referred to many as 'flying rats') even less likeable. With their drab colour, shabby appearance, bad diet and unacceptable toilet habits, they're the chavs of the bird world.

Pigeon sandwich

Another pigeon-related spot is the bread necklace. This occurs when the middle of a slice of bread is pecked away, leaving the crust intact, but in the process the slice flips up and lands around the bird's neck, making further consumption impossible.

Your eye-witness report

Fill out the form below and score points along the way.

Your notes

Log any other interesting observations below.

Location and date

Was there anything else wrong with the bird?

Dishevelled ◯   Broken wing(s) ◯   Dead ◯

Have you ever seen a pigeon ...   ... poo on someone? ◯

... fly into a window? ◯   ... wearing a bread necklace? ◯

What are your thoughts about pigeons?

Like ◯   Dislike ◯

Pet ◯   Pest ◯

Draw your subject's foot condition and markings.   Dinner ◯

How did you score?

1½ feet ☼5   1 foot ☼10   ½ foot ☼15   0 feet ☼20

TASK Catch the pigeon   I got a snap of me and the bird together ... ☼25   ... I got the bird to perch on me. ☼50

Final score

Spot a battle against the wind

Award points for:

5 A wayward umbrella

10 A newspaper lashing or dispossession

15 A clothing attack or desertion

20 A dismounting or flooring

TASK

Singing in the rain

Embrace the elements with a rain dance.

War on the world

At some point in the year, we'll all have to face some kind of head-to-head battle with the weather, and it won't be a fair fight. The elements pack a weighty arsenal behind them, including sun, snow, rain, hail, thunder, lightning, and, of course, wind – all of which can be wielded with targeted potency and in ruthless combinations.

In extreme wintry conditions a short walk can turn into an epic journey as people perform acrobatic manouevres in an effort to stay upright on the ice. In the aftermath of torrential rain, you may spot a pedestrian being soaked by a sheet of water thrown up from the wheels of a passing car. But the most common battles take place against the wind, the stealthiest and most mischievous of the elements.

The wind can steal your possessions, run off with your hat, play havoc with your hair and turn your defences against you. With one gust, an umbrella can flip inside out, baring its spokes, a newspaper can leap up, temporarily blinding its reader. Even clothing can turn turncoat and desert, or lash out against its wearer. Regularly tag-teaming with the rain, the wind can both drench and dry, uplift and downcast. It may lunge, snatch, thrust and finally wrestle its opponent to the floor.

CAPTURE THE MOMENT
OR DRAW WHAT YOU SAW

Vs.

Your eye-witness report

Fill out the form below and score points along the way.

Your notes

Log any other interesting observations below.

Location and date

Who did this happen to?

What was the weather like?

How strong was the wind?

Gentle   2   3   4   5   6   7   Gale force

Who ultimately won the battle?   The weather ◯   The person ◯   Neither ◯

How did you score?

Umbrella 5   News-paper 10   Clothing 15   Flooring 20

TASK Singing in the rain   I danced in the rain ... 25   ... naked 50

Final score

Spot a prank

Award points for:

5 Classic prank, e.g. coin glued to floor, rude note stuck to someone's back

10 Workplace high jinks, e.g. a prank call, a sabotaged computer or chair

15 A media hoax

20 A public show-stopper, e.g. a tampered statue, a car on a building

TASK

Pranks very much

Design your own original prank.

Dirty tricks

Who needs enemies when you have so-called friends? A friend with prankster tendencies can soon turn frenemy, but even those without the instinct may see an unattended Facebook page, for example, as an opportunity too good to miss for a laugh at someone else's expense.

In the world of practical jokers, students reign supreme, having the time, the energy and the passion for mischief needed for such dark arts. They specialise in everything from the opportunistic drawing of moustaches and obscenities on the faces of inebriated comrades, to highly engineered feats, such as leaving cars on the tops of buildings.

But you may also spot the handiwork of an office prankster, who choses to spice up a colleague's day with fake phone calls, super-glued stationery or sabotaged chairs and computers. You may see a sign that has been tampered with – you may even fall prey to one, and stride boldly into the wrong toilet. It's possible you might witness or fall victim to a prank set up by one of the many TV shows devoted to practical joke entertainment. If there's a time to be on top alert, though, it's got to be April 1. Scour the news for hoax reports and keep your wits about you wherever you go.

CAPTURE THE MOMENT
OR DRAW WHAT YOU SAW

Your eye-witness report

Fill out the form below and score points along the way.

Your notes

Log any other interesting observations below.

Location and date

Who was the prankster (mark 'P') and who was the victim (mark 'V')? Describe what happened.

What props were involved?

How did you score?

Classic 5   Work-place 10   Media hoax 15   Public show-stopper 20

TASK Pranks very much   My victim hated the prank. 25   My victim loved/tolerated my prank. 50

Final score

Spot something you've dreamt about

Award points for:

5 Déjà do

10 Déjà go

15 Déjà meet

20 Déjà win

TASK

Living the dream

Make a dream come true.

Sorry, can you repeat yourself?

The French phrase 'déjà vu' translates as 'already seen'. There are still no conclusive answers as to what it is or why it happens, but it can feel like you're reliving a dream. In some cases, perhaps you are.

A dream about going to buy some milk isn't the sort you're likely to remember or want to leap out of bed to write down, but it might come back to haunt you and, when it does, prepare to be amazed if a certain detail – for example, a red car passing by – suddenly gives you the sense you've already had this precise experience. It's often during mundane activities like this that déjà vu can strike. Points are available for going to new places or meeting new people you've dreamed about or recall with a strong sense of déjà vu. But the top points are awarded for predicting major events. If you can recall your premonition early enough, there could even be money to be made down at the bookies.

It's groundhog day ... again

According to *Groundhog Day* director, Harold Ramis, Phil Connors (the character played by Bill Murray) is trapped in the same day for about ten years. Other estimates range from 30 to 10,000 years.

CAPTURE THE MOMENT
OR DRAW WHAT YOU SAW

PAST & PRESENT

DEJA VU

PRESENT & PAST

Your eye-witness report

Fill out the form below and score points along the way.

Your notes

Log any other interesting observations below.

Location and date

What did you dream about?

And what actually happened in real life?

How did you score?

Déjà do 5   Déjà go 10   Déjà meet 15   Déjà win 20

TASK Living the dream | I made my own dream come true. 25 | I made someone else's dream come true. 50

Final score

Spot a bad hair day

Award points for:

5 Bad hair care

10 Bad hairstyle

15 Hair malfunction

20 Hair escape

TASK

It Will Grow Back*

Relive a hairstyle from your youth.

Hair peace

Sometimes it's as though your hair got out of the wrong side of bed. For no good reason it can't be controlled or reasoned with. The chances are no one will notice but you, so on the scale of hair crimes a straight bit that won't wave or a wavy bit that won't straighten is hardly going to alert the fashion police. The long and short of it is that, arguably, some hairstyles are just not great. Mullets, perms, bowls and comb-overs are hard for the most beautiful people to pull off. Other styles can be great, but require expert handling, not a DIY job, such as dreads, braids, perms, shaves and fringes. The same goes for colour. Look out for home-made bleaching blunders and green-tinged tresses.

Big hair can overshadow a face. For some, their uber long locks are paraded like show dogs, combed within an inch of their lives; for others, they are neglected, malnourished and begging for the snip. But it's not all about poor decisions and handling. A bad hairstyle can easily be born from a good one. All it takes is some added natural ingredients, like rain or wind, and a beehive can instantly be whipped into a birds' nest. The daddy of all hair crimes, though, is the toupee. Intended to disguise the fact that the wearer is lacking in the top-floor department, they so often draw attention to it. Be bald and be proud.

---

* It Will Grow Back was the name of a hair salon on Kingsland Road, London.

Your eye-witness report

Fill out the form below and score points along the way.

Your notes

Log any other interesting observations below.

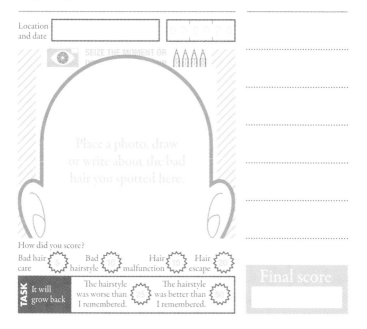

Location and date

DATE TIME

SEIZE THE MOMENT OR DRAW FROM MEMORY

Place a photo, draw or write about the bad hair you spotted here.

How did you score?

Bad hair care 5   Bad hairstyle 10   Hair malfunction 15   Hair escape 20

TASK It will grow back   The hairstyle was worse than I remembered. 25   The hairstyle was better than I remembered. 50

Final score

....

....

....

....

....

....

Spot a good deed

Award points for:

 Community spirit, e.g. guerilla gardening, litter picking

 Generosity, e.g. giving money, a lift, or giving up a place in a queue

 Helping hand, e.g. assisting the lost, frail, distressed, stranded and injured

 Protecting or saving someone's life (including animals)

TASK

Do-gooder

Perform your own good deed.

In deed

Gone is the time when helping a pensioner cross a busy road was the default good deed. Today's sprightly pensioners are more likely to mow you down in motors at a crossing or jump the lights on their fixed gear bike than stand helplessly on the curb watching the traffic go by.

A good deed is any selfless act of kindness, so the range is wide. Of course, the vast majority will be impossible to spot, as they happen out of sight or involve decisions to donate resources or volunteer service. And those random and spontaneous acts of street kindness that do occur will be hard to anticipate, but when you see one you will feel instantly uplifted – and possibly shamed or inspired.

So be alert to everyday benefactions: from community-spirited actions, like picking up litter, to kind considerations, like giving up a seat on a bus, to more out-of-the way charitableness, such as pushing a stranger's broken-down car, chasing the owner of some forgotten item or reuniting a lost child with their carer. You may even come across one of those people who go beyond good Samaritan to guardian angel, the sort who don't give a thought to stepping into a situation, however dangerous, in order to protect a fellow human being.

CAPTURE THE MOMENT
OR DRAW WHAT YOU SAW

THE AWARD FOR A

RANDOM ACT OF KINDNESS

GOES TO

FOR

Your eye-witness report

Fill out the form below and score points along the way.

Location and date

Who helped whom? Tick and specify in the box ...

What happened?

How did you score?

Community spirit **5** Gener-osity **10** Helping hand **15** Life-saving **20**

TASK I did a good deed ... ... for someone I know. **25** ... for a complete stranger. **50**

Your notes

Log any other interesting observations below.

Final score

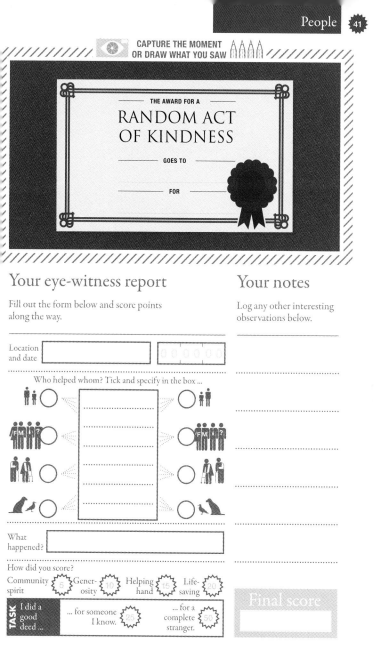

Spot the inexplicable

Award points for:

- **5** Spotting an inexplicable phenomenon
- **10** Spotting it in the presence of another witness
- **15** Spotting it and having physical proof, e.g. photo
- **20** All of the above

TASK

Hoax

Fake a photo of an extraterrestrial or super-natural phenomenon.

Super un-natural

Science brings us an ever greater understanding of the world around us, but there continue to be mysteries that defy rational explanation. Take strange lights in the sky, for example. While most sightings can be put down to misidentified man-made objects, or natural or astronomical phenomena, a significant minority remain unidentified. Given the size of the universe, it doesn't seem possible for the human race to be the only form of intelligent life out there. From the discovery of odd cave paintings and ancient artefacts with coded writing, to crop and stone circles, people have been spotting possible signs of alien communication for centuries.

Others have spotted strange beasts. Cryptids are creatures whose existence isn't yet recognised by science, such as the Loch Ness monster and the Yeti. Dragons, werewolves and unicorns are among the other cryptids that have long been the subject of folklore and study. There is also a lot of documentation on the paranormal: ghosts, poltergeists, telepathy, ESP, spiritual healing, out-of-body experiences, prophecy and demonic possession. So keep your spotting eye open to extreme possibilities. The more evidence you can gather of your sighting, the more points you get.

Your eye-witness report

Fill out the form below and score points along the way.

| Location and date | | 0 0 0 0 0 0 |

CAPTURE THE MOMENT OR DRAW WHAT YOU SAW 🎃🎃🎃🎃

Place a photograph, a drawing or a description of what you saw here.

How did you score?

Inexplicable 〈5〉 Plus witness 〈10〉 Plus proof 〈15〉 All 〈20〉

TASK Hoax | My fake photo didn't fool anyone. 〈25〉 | My fake photo fooled someone! 〈50〉

Your notes

Log any other interesting observations below.

....

....

....

....

....

....

Final score

Spot an _identical or odd_ couple

Award points for:

5 Similar clothing

10 Similar clothing and physique

15 Opposites in style

20 Opposites in style and physique

TASK

Perfect match

Set up a date between two very similar friends and two different ones.

Peas in a pod

Though it has often been said that opposites attract, the opposite is probably closer to the truth. A number of studies have shown that it is similarity, not only in tastes and interests but in looks, that attracts people to each other, with men and women tending to seek out more masculine or feminine versions of themselves.

This being true, spotting an identical couple may not be as hard as it sounds, and may be easier than spotting a truly odd couple. Some couples stand out by being dressed in a similar way too – occasionally even in matching outfits. And it's not just partners who do this – it can be friends, family members or work colleagues. When it comes to the odd couple, there are many ways to be different, so you're looking for the pair that makes you think, 'So how does that work?'

Double take

Look out for those embarrassing fashion coincidences, in which people discover they are wearing the same outfit as a fellow party guest. Do they team up and have a laugh about it or spend the night trying to maintain a discreet distance from their twin clothes horse?

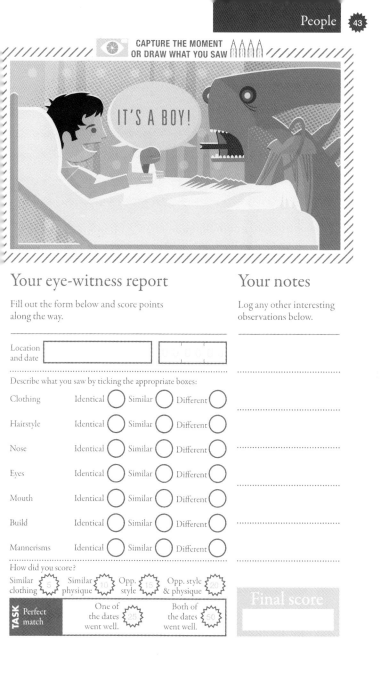

Your eye-witness report

Fill out the form below and score points along the way.

Your notes

Log any other interesting observations below.

Location and date		

Describe what you saw by ticking the appropriate boxes:

Clothing	Identical ◯	Similar ◯	Different ◯
Hairstyle	Identical ◯	Similar ◯	Different ◯
Nose	Identical ◯	Similar ◯	Different ◯
Eyes	Identical ◯	Similar ◯	Different ◯
Mouth	Identical ◯	Similar ◯	Different ◯
Build	Identical ◯	Similar ◯	Different ◯
Mannerisms	Identical ◯	Similar ◯	Different ◯

How did you score?

Similar clothing 5   Similar physique 10   Opp. style 15   Opp. style & physique 20

TASK Perfect match   One of the dates went well. 25   Both of the dates went well. 50

Final score

Spot an optical illusion

Award points for:

5 Staged with a camera

10 Naturally occurring illusion

15 Unconvincing 3D street art

20 Convincing 3D street art

TASK

The camera lies

Set up and photograph your own optical illusion.

Objects in the mirror are closer than they appear

There are lots of kinds of optical illusion, and you can often chance across them by looking in the right direction at the right moment. Clouds might masquerade as mountains; long distances may appear short, large objects as small (or vice versa); reflections may convince you something is there when it is not; faces may appear in strange places (see No. 29); and painted or patterned surfaces may seem to be moving or three-dimensional. Printed scaffolding covers, for example, might fool you into seeing the building hidden beneath.

A current trend in street art is to create a drawing on the pavement which, when viewed from a certain angle, looks three-dimensional. This unnerving form of illusion has been employed by officials in West Vancouver to create an unusual speeding deterrent: a forced perspective image of a girl chasing a ball in the middle of the road.*

Optical illusions can be created by anyone using a camera and a bit of devious perspective. The simplest of all is picking the sun or moon out of the sky with your fingers, or holding large but faraway objects in the palm of your hand. But the daddy of them all is holding up the leaning tower of Pisa with your bare hands. Easy Pisa.

....

* It can be seen here on You Tube: http://goo.gl/hVNLN

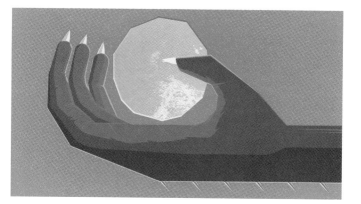

Your eye-witness report

Fill out the form below and score points along the way.

Location and date		0 0 0 0

📷 **CAPTURE THE MOMENT OR DRAW WHAT YOU SAW** 🖐🖐🖐🖐

How did you score?

Photo-graphic ⟨5⟩ Natural ⟨10⟩ Uncon-vincing ⟨15⟩ Convin-cing ⟨20⟩

TASK The camera lies | My illusion was unconvincing. ⟨25⟩ | My illusion was very convincing. ⟨50⟩

Your notes

Log any other interesting observations below.

....

....

....

....

....

....

Final score

Spot a public meltdown

Award points for:

 5 Shouting and swearing

 10 Tears and tantrums

 15 Physical aggression

20 All of the above

TASK

Sorry statement

Make a public apology to someone you've upset.

Angrifying

In a world of labour-saving technologies, public transportation, food on the go and pocket devices that provide information at our fingertips, you'd think that modern life would be a stress-free utopia. Wrong. As we become more obsessed with efficiency and convenience, so our pace of life has accelerated to the point where our patience, attention span and tolerance of others is frequently tested to the limit. Small, everyday annoyances can build up and take us to breaking point. Tears, tantrums and ridiculous confrontations can then ensue.

According to a poll by Ordissimo, the five most infuriating things about modern life are self-service checkouts, bad driving, cold calling, junk mail and computer malfunctions.* Another poll on intolerance by Lactofree highlighted other major annoyances, including: people who talk loudly on their phones, people who walk painfully slowly on the street or drive slowly in the fast lane, noisy neighbours, cashiers who give you your change on top of a receipt, iPhone obsessives and queue jumpers.† And it's not only strangers that can push us over the edge. Our nearest and dearest – parents, children, siblings, partners and friends – are experts at knowing which buttons to press, so you may witness a fair amount of dirty laundry being aired in public too.

* Poll carried out November 2012 • † Poll carried out September 2009

CAPTURE THE MOMENT
OR DRAW WHAT YOU SAW

Your eye-witness report

Fill out the form below and score points along the way.

Your notes

Log any other interesting observations below.

Location and date

| 0 0 0 0 0 0 |

Who lost it?

○ ○ ○ ○ ○ ○ ○ ○ ○

What were they upset about?

Bad service ○ Bad behaviour ○ Bad news ○ I don't know ○

Who or what bore the brunt of their meltdown?

How did it end?

Peaceful resolution ○ Storming off ○ Third-party intervention ○ I didn't see ○

How did you score?

Shouting & swearing ⟨5⟩ Tears & tantrums ⟨10⟩ Physical aggression ⟨15⟩ All ⟨20⟩

TASK I made a public apology .... but it didn't work. ⟨25⟩ ... and all was forgiven! ⟨50⟩

Final score

Spot an 'X' in the sky made by vapour trails

Award points for:

 5 A plane vapour trail 'X'

 10 Trails from aerobatic displays, e.g. the Red Arrows

 15 Legible skywriting, e.g. 'Will you marry me?' or advertising

 20 A natural cloud 'X' (or any other letter)

TASK

Flyover

Spot a flock of birds flying in a 'V' formation.

Plane sailing

With thousands of planes flying in the sky above at any given moment, it's only a matter of time before two planes cross each other's flight paths to create the perfect sky 'X'.

The vapour trails you see overhead don't occur every time a plane flies across the sky, though: the atmospheric conditions need to be just right. Much depends on the temperature and humidity of the surrounding air: it must be cold enough for the vapour to condense, and the higher the humidity, the longer the trails will last. This is why some days you see planes without any trails and on other days the sky resembles a piece of blue paper with children's scribbles all over it. Keep your eyes peeled at all times, including when you're in a plane, and also try to spot a natural cloud 'X' (see No. 3).

Skywriting is so last century

Instead of one acrobatic plane spelling words one letter at a time, in skytyping five planes do the same job, working like a dot matrix printer by flying in formation and emitting puffs of computer controlled vapour over a distance of five miles. Fast, effective and legible.

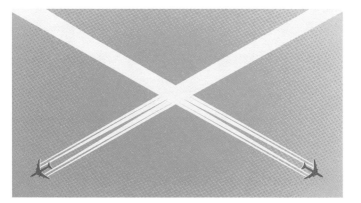

Your eye-witness report

Fill out the form below and score points along the way.

| Location and date | | |

CAPTURE THE MOMENT OR DRAW WHAT YOU SAW

How did you score?

Plane 'X' — 5   Aero-batics — 10   Sky-writing — 15   Natural cloud 'X' — 20

TASK Flyover — I spotted a flock in a 'V' formation. — 25   I spotted a 'W' formation (two 'V's together). — 50

Your notes

Log any other interesting observations below.

....

....

....

....

....

....

Final score

Spot a moment of pure slapstick

Award points for:

5 A smile-inducing incident

10 A giggle-inducing gaff

15 A hearty-laugh-inducing routine

20 A LMAO performance (and keep laughing each time you remember it)

TASK

Kings of comedy

Invent a slapstick routine to amuse your kids or your friends's kids.

Fall guy

It takes a brilliant actor, like Chaplin, to perform slapstick well, but in real life it is all too easy to do without any effort whatsoever. The most ordinary situations prove to be the most hazardous. Falling up kerbs, standing on rakes, tripping over bollards or uneven paving stones, walking up the down escalator or into lamp posts and glass doors, misjudging distances, struggling with deck chairs and other collapsible items, skidding on floor food or tipping a drink over one's crotch (see No. 26): most of these situations are completely avoidable if you're paying enough attention. But our obsession with doing more than one thing at the same time continuously threatens to set us up for a joke at our own expense. Still, at least with a slapstick accident any onlookers will be entertained, and – assuming no one gets seriously hurt – a healthy dose of laughter will usually help the victim recover.

Text alert

In 2011, CCTV captured the moment a woman fell into a fountain in a US shopping mall as she texted. Texting while walking has increased the potential for street slapstick, but a number of serious accidents have led to 'text tripping' being banned in some places in the USA.

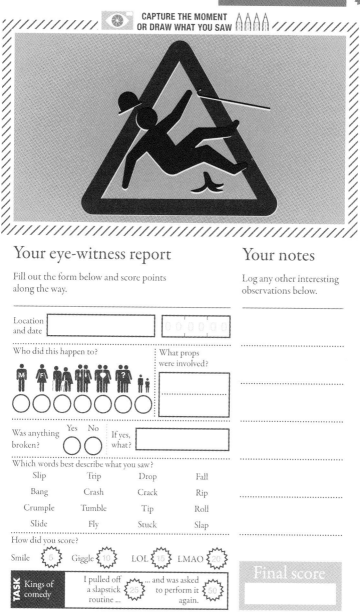

CAPTURE THE MOMENT
OR DRAW WHAT YOU SAW

Your eye-witness report

Fill out the form below and score points along the way.

Location and date | 0 0 0 0 0 0

Who did this happen to?

What props were involved?

Was anything broken? Yes No — If yes, what?

Which words best describe what you saw?

Slip	Trip	Drop	Fall
Bang	Crash	Crack	Rip
Crumple	Tumble	Tip	Roll
Slide	Fly	Stuck	Slap

How did you score?

Smile 5 — Giggle 10 — LOL 15 — LMAO 20

TASK Kings of comedy — I pulled off a slapstick routine 25 ... and was asked to perform it again. 50

Your notes

Log any other interesting observations below.

Final score

Spot a film set in action

Award points for:

 5 A famous ex-film location

10 A TV report being shot

 15 A film or TV set with production crew

20 Lights, camera, action!

TASK

Extra! Extra!

See a film in production from the inside by becoming an extra.

Lights ... camera ... action

There are lots of independent film and TV producers out there, so the chances of stumbling across a set in action might be better than you think. With blockbusters, though, come big budgets, big names and secrecy – tracking them down may require a bit of homework first.

Check the Internet for movie-related news and gossip. There are websites that can point you in the right direction for films in production near you. The press love it when a celebrity is in town, so you'll often be able to track down a set by keeping a tab on the local news. And if a blockbuster does come to your part of the world, they may need some average Joe's and Josephine's to make up the numbers in a crowd scene or to litter a WWII battlefield, giving you the opportunity to see a film set in action from the inside out.

New York: film set city

With guidebooks to hundreds of old movie locations and great websites, with maps updated daily, to take you to current ones (e.g. www.screentours.com/whats-filming-now), spinning by a set or two in the world's most filmed city shouldn't be too hard.

CAPTURE THE MOMENT
OR DRAW WHAT YOU SAW

INSERT CGI HERE

Your eye-witness report

Fill out the form below and score points along the way.

Your notes

Log any other interesting observations below.

Location and date

What was being filmed?

TV ◯ Film ◯ Sci-fi ◯ Fantasy ◯ Comedy ◯

Drama ◯ Adventure ◯ Documentary ◯ Not sure ◯

Title of the production (if known)

Did you see anyone famous?   Yes ◯   No ◯   If yes, who?

What did you see?

Trailers ◯ Hair and make-up ◯ Sound equipment ◯ Cameras ◯

Actors ◯ Lights ◯ Filming ◯ Director ◯

How did you score?

Ex-film location ⭐5   TV report ⭐10   TV/Film set (no action) ⭐15   Filming a scene ⭐20

TASK Extra! Extra!   I got a job as an extra ... ⭐25   ... and was given a line to say. ⭐50

Final score

Spot a ___cat___ with a ___moustache___

Award points for:

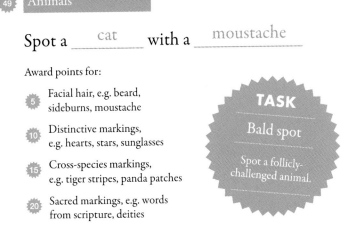

- **5** Facial hair, e.g. beard, sideburns, moustache
- **10** Distinctive markings, e.g. hearts, stars, sunglasses
- **15** Cross-species markings, e.g. tiger stripes, panda patches
- **20** Sacred markings, e.g. words from scripture, deities

TASK

Bald spot

Spot a follicly-challenged animal.

Fur style

With a well-shaped and well-placed patch of coloured fur, feathers or skin, animals can appear to be sporting moustaches, beards, eye patches, quirky hairstyles, sunglasses or even love hearts.

When it comes to animals with distinctive markings, it's not all about cats that look like Hitler. With natural markings in the right places, some animals can end up resembling a different species altogether: dogs have been seen with markings that make them look like cows; cows have been spotted with markings that make them look like pandas. Various types of animal all around the world have been found with religious words or symbols emblazoned on their bodies, some even with the actual image of a deity, making them prized pets and, often, sacred cows.

New look

If you're bored with your dog, then you could take inspiration from the Chinese craze of dyeing pet dogs to look like more exotic species. Your dog's fur may be dyed to make it look like a tiger or a panda, or it can be groomed in the style of a camel or horse.

Your eye-witness report

Fill out the form below and score points along the way.

Location and date [   ] [0 0 0 0 0 0]

⊙ **CAPTURE THE MOMENT OR DRAW WHAT YOU SAW**

How did you score?

Facial hair {5} Distinctive {10} Cross-species {15} Sacred {20}

TASK **Bald spot** | I saw a partially bald animal. {25} | I saw a completely hairless animal. {50}

Your notes

Log any other interesting observations below.

....

....

....

....

....

....

Final score

[   ]

See a lightning strike

Award points for:

5 Cloud-to-cloud or sheet lightning

10 A strike from a distance (strike point not seen)

15 A strike on an object

20 Ground-to-cloud or ball lightning

TASK

Lightning speed

Capture a lightning flash on camera.

Strike you down

With an estimated two thousand thunderstorms happening globally at any one time, and up to a hundred lightning flashes every second, it sounds like it should be easy to spot a lightning strike. But most lightning doesn't extend beyond the thundercloud it comes from, and if it does, the next most likely place it goes is to another cloud.

Your best chance of seeing a lightning strike is to watch a lightning rod on a tall building during a storm. The Empire State Building is struck by lightning around 20–100 times a year. The Vatican also receives a lot of strikes, and was famously struck when Pope Benedict announced his resignation in 2013. Mountains, trees and towers are also prime targets for strikes as the lightning looks for the easiest route to the Earth. Occasionally a tall object on the ground will trigger a lightning strike upwards. Extra points are awarded for spotting this or any other rare lightning events, such as mysterious ball lightning.

Lightning can strike anything, though, not only tall objects, and sometimes in the same spot more than once. So stay indoors during a storm. The following activities are very dangerous: standing beneath a tree, playing golf, climbing a mountain or fishing in open water.

Your eye-witness report

Fill out the form below and score points along the way.

Location and date	

How close to the lightning strike were you?
Very far ◯ Quite far ◯ Quite close ◯ Too close ◯

Did you see what the lightning struck? Yes ◯ No ◯ If yes, what did it strike?

A building or tower ◯ A tree ◯ A statue ◯ A vehicle ◯ An animal ◯ A person ◯

If other, what?

How much damage did it cause?
None ◯ A little ◯ Sub-stantial ◯ A lot ◯

How did you score?

Cloud-to-cloud	Distant strike	Object strike	Ground-to-cloud or ball
5	10	15	20

TASK Lightning speed
I captured a lightning flash. 25 I captured a lightning strike. 50

Your notes

Log any other interesting observations below.

....

....

....

....

....

Final score

Spot lost treasure

Award points for:

- **5** £10–£49 (or item of similar value)

- **10** £50–£100 (or item of similar value)

- **15** More than £100 (or item of similar value)

- **20** Priceless, e.g. a museum piece, a child's toy, a wedding ring

TASK

Give it away

Find lost valuables and return them to their owner.

Pocket the money

Chances are you're not going to win the lottery, discover your long-lost uncle has left you a fortune or be gifted a share of billions of dollars (in exchange for a small fee) by that the foreign prince who emailed you out of the blue. But, every now and again, we get a little lucky and chance across some hidden or lost treasure. Leave the pennies and dimes for the kids: what's needed here is a decent wad of dosh, a whole bunch of big ones or an item of substantial value. Perhaps it's been dropped on the street, or left behind in a bar, or maybe you'll uncover it in a car boot sale, in the attic, or buried in the garden.

The trouble is, what you find might not always be yours to keep, which presents you with a dilemma. For wherever there's a finder-keeper, somewhere there's a loser-weeper.

Priceless

Certain things are simply irreplaceable and one person's rubbish may be another person's treasure. Items of sentimental value, such as a child's toy or a handed-down trinket, will be worth much more to the owner than to anyone else.

Your eye-witness report

Fill out the form below and score points along the way.

Your notes

Log any other interesting observations below.

Location and date [   ] [0 0 0 0 0]

///// WHAT / HOW MUCH DID YOU FIND? /////

Did you keep it?   Yes ◯   No ◯   If no, what did you do with it? [   ]

If yes, what did you spend it on? [   ]

How did you score?

£10-£49 ✺5   £50-£100 ✺10   More than £100 ✺15   Priceless ✺20

TASK Give it away   I tried to find the owner but failed. ✺25   I found the owner and returned their treasure. ✺50

Final score [   ]

....

....

....

....

....

....

Spot someone's double

Award points for:

 5 Same hair

 10 Same facial features

 15 Same physique

 20 All of the above

TASK

Mistaken identity

If you are mistaken for someone else, play along for as long as you can.

I no you

Unless you've got an identical twin, you probably like to think you're one of a kind. But with the billions of people living on this planet, there's bound to be at least one person out there who's the spitting image of you or someone you know. You just haven't spotted them yet.

Cases of mistaken identity happen all the time, thanks to the huge numbers of almost-alikes out there. Almost-alikes are people who, from a distance or behind, bear a striking resemblance to someone you know, but close up turn out to be like a distorted photocopy of the person you thought they were. As an avatar version won't do, you'll need to search long and hard for a real doppelgänger. Fellas, always keep a look out for your brother-from-another-mother; ladies, it's a sister-from-another-mister for you.

Family members don't count

While the easiest place to spot your doppelgänger might be a family gathering – perhaps you look the spitting image of your mum – that's cheating. Search further afield. And if you're lucky enough to have an identical twin, keep an eye out for an unrelated triplet.

CAPTURE THE MOMENT
OR DRAW WHAT YOU SAW

Your eye-witness report

Fill out the form below and score points along the way.

Location and date

Who did they look like?

Did you ...   ... spot him/her from afar? ◯   ... spot him/her in a photograph? ◯   ... meet him/her? ◯

Ring the characteristics they shared.

Eyes	Nose	Mouth	Ears
Hair	Bone structure	Height	Build
Glasses	Clothes	Shoes	Accessories
Voice	Laugh	Humour	Personality
Mannerisms	Gait	Hands	Feet

How did you score?

Hair style 5   Facial features 10   Physique 15   All 20

TASK Mistaken identity   I tried but I couldn't convince them. 25   They fell for it. I'm also known as 50

Your notes

Log any other interesting observations below.

Final score

Spot a memorable wedding moment

Award points for:

5 Good

10 Bad

15 Ugly

20 All of the above

TASK

Will you marry me?

Spot a public marriage proposal.

The good, the bad and the ugly

The good – Fortunately most weddings are great, but they can be formulaic affairs too. To be memorably good, something needs to be incredibly spectacular or spectacularly original. It could be the venue, dress, cake or vows, a special guest or performance, or a combination of personal touches, including a first dance worthy of YouTube.

The bad – An excruciating speech, with embarrassing photos, an unwelcome gatecrasher, a flatulent vicar, terrible weather, food poisoning, a clothes or prop malfunction: there's usually something that doesn't go according to plan, but hopefully these inconveniences and mishaps can be laughed off with time and remembered fondly.

The ugly – An emotional gathering of people consuming lots of free alcohol is a potential recipe for spectacular, though unscheduled, fireworks. The occasion may rekindle the jealousy of an ex or feuds between estranged family members, and singletons may turn predator and stalk unwilling victims. But it might not be the guests who misbehave. Some grooms or bridezillas will demand perfection on their big day and freak out if things fall short. Or else they may suffer cold feet and faint at the altar or fail to show at all.

Your eye-witness report

Fill out the form below and score points along the way.

Your notes

Log any other interesting observations below.

Location and date [   ] [0 0 0 0 0 0]

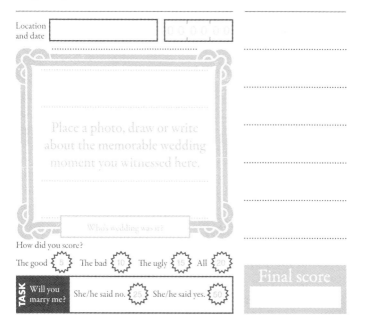

Place a photo, draw or write about the memorable wedding moment you witnessed here.

Who's wedding was it?

How did you score?

The good ☆ 5 ☆ The bad ☆ 10 ☆ The ugly ☆ 15 ☆ All ☆ 20 ☆

TASK Will you marry me? She/he said no. ☆ 25 ☆ She/he said yes. ☆ 50 ☆

Final score [   ]

Spot someone incognito

Award points for:

 5   Functional camouflage

10   Hide and seek

15   Hiding in plain sight, e.g. celebrities and criminals

20   A stake out, e.g. cops and paps

TASK

I'm watching you ...

Make eye contact with an incognitoist and make the 'I'm watching you' gesture.*

Coming ... ready or not

The problem with spotting someone incognito is that they're trying to be invisible. So other than stumbling across a game of hide-and-seek, who and what should you be looking for?

Criminals, troublemakers, celebrities and the socially awkward all have good reasons for not wishing to be noticed. They could appear as fast-moving, well-covered-up individuals, who avoid eye contact and occasionally duck into doorways or pretend to look into shop windows. Plain-clothes cops and photographers may act just as suspiciously when in pursuit of one of these people. In the case of paparazzi, their game of cat and mouse may take them on to rooftops, up trees or into bushes and bins.

But they're not the only ones keen not to be seen. If you've ever spotted someone in the street you're desperate not to talk to, had a massive zit on your face or a really bad hairdo you can't wait to sort out when you get home, then you will also know about keeping a low profile.

In the great outdoors, some of the people you see in camouflage might actually be wearing it for reasons other than fashion, so look out for hunters, paint-ballers and army folk on exercise.

---

* This gesture was made famous by Robert de Niro in Meet the Parents.

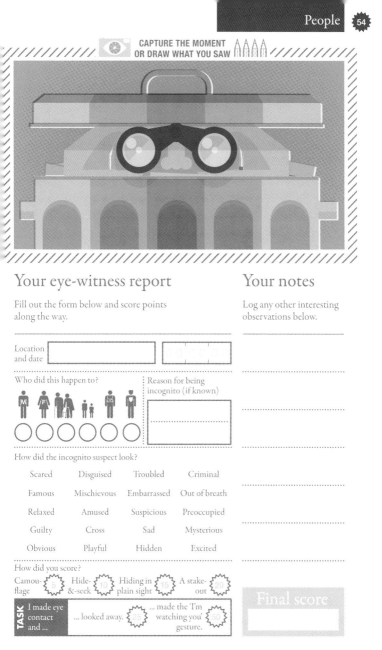

CAPTURE THE MOMENT OR DRAW WHAT YOU SAW

Your eye-witness report

Fill out the form below and score points along the way.

Location and date	

Who did this happen to?

○ ○ ○ ○ ○ ○

Reason for being incognito (if known)

How did the incognito suspect look?

Scared	Disguised	Troubled	Criminal
Famous	Mischievous	Embarrassed	Out of breath
Relaxed	Amused	Suspicious	Preoccupied
Guilty	Cross	Sad	Mysterious
Obvious	Playful	Hidden	Excited

How did you score?

Camouflage 5   Hide-&-seek 10   Hiding in plain sight 15   A stake-out 20

TASK I made eye contact and ... ... looked away. 25   ... made the 'I'm watching you' gesture. 30

Your notes

Log any other interesting observations below.

Final score

Spot something hanging on overhead wires

Award points for:

5 Footwear or clothing

10 Random objects, e.g. toys, headphones, a brace of pheasants

15 Guerilla art

20 A parachutist or hot-air balloonist

TASK

Start a shoe tree

Toss a pair of shoes into a tree and see if others do the same.

Throw up

Overhead wires have been attracting flora and fauna since they were first erected. Birds were quick to utilise them as places to rest and gather, while the flora got a piece of the action too, moving in with natural hanging baskets of epiphytic plants.* And then the unnatural got in on the act.

There is no definitive explanation as to how the tradition of shoe-tossing started. These days, seeing a pair of laced-together trainers hanging above you might signal anything from a practical joke, to the commemoration of a success or loss, or even to the proximity of a drug den or brothel. Much depends on where you see them. Most people probably do it for the sheer hell of it, to see what can be achieved by flinging objects, even art, bolas-style, into unreachable places.

Other footwear tossers ...

Wellie wanging is a sport originating in Yorkshire, UK, in which gumboots are thrown as far as possible. In other areas of the world, shoes are thrown as a sign of protest, George Bush being one of the most famous victims of a 'shoeing' during a 2008 press conference in Iraq.

---

* Also known as air plants, as they don't need to be rooted in soil but can survive off particles captured in the air.

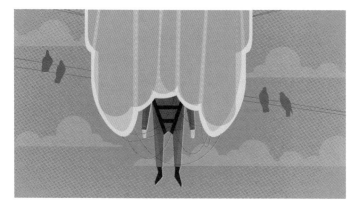

Your eye-witness report

Fill out the form below and score points along the way.

Location and date

⊙ CAPTURE THE MOMENT
OR DRAW WHAT YOU SAW

How did you score?

Shoes/clothes ⟨5⟩ Random ⟨10⟩ Guerilla art ⟨15⟩ Parachutist/balloonist ⟨20⟩

TASK Start a shoe tree

I tossed a pair of shoes into a tree ... ⟨25⟩ ... and now the tree has lots of shoes. ⟨50⟩

Your notes

Log any other interesting observations below.

....

....

....

....

....

....

Final score

Spot a criminal act (and someone thwarting it)

Award points for:

 5 A criminal act

 10 A police chase

 15 Arrest or apprehension by the police/security

 20 Arrest or apprehension by a civilian

TASK

In the name of the law

Make a citizen's arrest, like Batman here: http://goo.gl/tRIIs

Crime and punishment

Our modern society wouldn't be the same security-obsessed and paranoid place without a steady stream of sirens blaring, 24/7 panic-inducing news coverage and the inescapable CCTV cameras responsible for a constant film fest in which we're all unwitting extras.

There are estimated to be around 26,000 crimes every day in the UK alone.[*] That equates to approximately seventeen crimes every single minute, from the petty and victimless to the downright villainous. It's a wonder any of us leave the house at all. When you do, chances are you'll spot something illegal along the way. Hopefully you'll also see the criminal apprehended. Look out for security guards swooping down on a shoplifter, police chasing after a suspect or a pensioner taking down escaping robbers with her handbag.[†]

It's all fine

It's as well to be aware of the rules wherever you are. For example, you'll pay a penalty if you do the following: park against the flow of traffic in Australia; keep an unkempt lawn in the village of Massapequa Park, New York; and eat or drink near Rome's famous landmarks.

[*] Figures from the Office of National Statistics Crime Survey for England and Wales for the year ending Sept 2012.
[†] A seventy-one-year-old single-handedly took on a gang of robbers outside a jewellery shop in Northampton, UK, in 2011. Check out the footage on YouTube: http://goo.gl/7yQJR.

CAPTURE THE MOMENT
OR DRAW WHAT YOU SAW

ROSS **CAUTION ILLUSTRATION CRIME SCENE DO NOT CROS**

RNING **MOVE ALONG NOTHING TO SEE WARNING MOVE**

RIME SCENE **DO NOT CROSS CAUTION ILLUSTRATION CRI**

NG **NOTHING TO SEE WARNING MOVE ALONG NOTHING**

Your eye-witness report

Fill out the form below and score points along the way.

Your notes

Log any other interesting observations below.

Location and date

Who was the criminal?

What did they do?

How serious do you rate this crime?

A bit naughty — Bad — Serious — Very serious — Terrible

Did the criminal ...

... get away? ... get caught? ... get arrested? ... give themselves up? I didn't see

What did you do?

Call the police / Alert someone / Try to stop them / Act as witness / Nothing

How did you score?

Criminal act 5 / Chase 10 / Thwarted by police 15 / Thwarted by civilian 20

TASK I made a citizen's arrest ... ... but the criminal got away. 25 ... and I handed them over to the police. 50

Final score

Spot someone on their way to a fancy-dress party

Award points for:

 5 Halloween party-goers

 10 Stag and hen parties

 15 Stag and hen parties

20 Random party guest

TASK

Suits you

Get a photograph of yourself with the costumed person.

Fancy that!

Spotting a costumed person in everyday life is easy if you know where to look, but spotting an out-of-context fancy-dressed guest is more a matter of luck. Most fancy-dressed guests probably opt for a taxi so as not to draw attention to themselves, but may lose their inhibitions after a night of drinking and brave the streets or public transport system. So keep your eyes peeled – it would be easy to miss a couple of bearded ladies sitting behind you on the bus or a man walking past you in a dress. The classic after-life party guest could be so convincing as their famous deceased celebrity, you mistake them for the real thing. Togas, robots, superheroes, devils and the like should be much more conspicuous.

You're far more likely to spot a flock of hens or a herd of stags staggering by, either all in some form of costume, good or bad, or accompanying the dressed-up bride- or groom-to-be. You may also chance across a competitor on their way to or from a fun run, or a trekkie or wookie on their way to a convention.

Failing all the above, you're guaranteed to see a few ghosts, cats, witches and zombies wandering around in fancy dress at Halloween.

**CAPTURE THE MOMENT
OR DRAW WHAT YOU SAW**

Your eye-witness report

Fill out the form below and score points
along the way.

Your notes

Log any other interesting
observations below.

Location
and date

Could you tell who or what the person
was dressed up as?   Yes ◯ No ◯

If yes, what?

Rate the craftsmanship of the costume you saw:

Terrible   Poor   OK   Good   Awesome

What was the costumed
person doing when you
spotted them?

How did the fancy-dressed guest look?

Embarrassed ◯ Confident ◯ Drunk ◯ Couldn't ◯
tell

How did you score?

Halloween ✦5✦ Stag or ✦10✦ Fun ✦15✦ Random ✦20✦
hen party   run   party

TASK Suits you I got a photo ✦25✦ ... and I ✦30✦
with them ...   crashed
their party.

Final score

Spot a bad tattoo

Award points for:

5   Bad subject matter

10   Bad placement

15   Execution

20   All

TASK

Ink about it

Design your own tattoo.

Tat-who?

Lying somewhere between art and fashion, tattoos, like both, are simply a matter of opinion. Or to put it another way, there's no accounting for taste. A bad tattoo for one person might be a work of art to another. However, there will always be some areas of general consensus. So, when looking for your tattoo, consider the following:

Bad subject matter: This includes pretend wounds, pretend facial hair, any kind of explicit stuff, baby portraits, pretentious wording and giant lifelike spiders. The list goes on (see below).

Bad placement: To many people, any sort of facial tattoo will seem like a bad idea, but a teardrop on the cheek is one thing, a pair of eyes on the eyelids another – and a full-head balaclava quite another still. And there's really nothing to say about a breast inked on each knee.

Bad execution: Poorly drawn portraits have to be the worst. In the wrong hands, Lady Gaga could end up like Lady Jabba, and Freddie Mercury like Freddy Krueger. Also look out for bad grammar, bad spelling, bad translations and badly executed fonts. A tattoo shouldn't look like something your mates drew on you when you were pissed.

LIVE WITHOUT REGETS

Your eye-witness report

Fill out the form below and score points along the way.

Your notes

Log any other interesting observations below.

Location and date

CAPTURE THE MOMENT
OR DRAW WHAT YOU SAW

....

....

....

....

....

....

How did you score?

| Subject matter | 5 | Placement | 10 | Execution | 15 | All | 20 |

| TASK | Ink about it | I designed my own ... | 25 | ... and I got it inked on. | 50 |

Final score

Spot someone go against the flow

Award points for:

 5 A free radical

10 A crowdzilla

15 A wrong wayfairer

20 A travelator gladiator

TASK

This way up

Take the escalator challenge, and run up the down or down the up.

Flow away

In a heavily populated and fast-moving world, it's generally easier to go with the flow than fight against it. But sometimes you'll spot an individual who's made the decision to be different, to cut through the tide of flowbots with a flow of their own, or who, through accident, drunkenness or stupidity, finds themselves swimming upstream. Here are some examples to look out for:

Free radicals – people who stand out from the crowd by refusing to conform with established or accepted customs, beliefs or attitudes. These include vogueons, who have a fashion sense entirely their own.

Crowdzillas – people who force their way through large crowds going in the opposite direction to them.

Wrong wayfarers – people who drive on the wrong side of the road or the wrong way down a one-way street.

Travelator gladiators – people who literally go against the flow by attempting to walk up or down an escalator or travelator the wrong way. Alcohol may be fuelling this act.

CAPTURE THE MOMENT
OR DRAW WHAT YOU SAW

Your eye-witness report

Fill out the form below and score points
along the way.

Your notes

Log any other interesting
observations below.

Location
and date

Who defied the flow?

M F

What kind of flow did they defy?

Fashion ◯   Custom ◯

Opinion ◯   Beliefs ◯

Traffic ◯   Escalator ◯

Crowd ◯   Travelator ◯

Which words would you use to describe their attempt?

A failure	Pointless	Courageous	Successful
Amusing	Anarchic	Foolish	Skilful
Lucky	Eccentric	Trendsetting	Slow
Exhausting	Embarrassing	Illegal	Political

How did you score?

Free radical ✦5   Crowd-zilla ✦10   Wrong wayfarer ✦15   Travelator gladiator ✦20

TASK I took the escalator challenge ...   ... and failed. ✦25   ... and succeeded. ✦50

Final score

Spot a lost tourist

Award points for:

 Identifying a lost soul

 Offering to help

 Accompanying them
some/all of the way

20 All of the above and doing
it in the tourist's native language

TASK

Say 'Fromage!'

Take a photo
for a tourist.

Not from round here

Tourists are usually easy to spot, with their bum bags, enormous cameras, ill-fitting shorts and rucksacks over-filled with guide books and strange-looking foreign snacks. Sometimes they can be found in groups, following a guide with a brightly coloured umbrella.

Spotting a lost tourist is harder. You may be able to attract one in a tourist hot spot, like a station or city square, simply by looking approachable and well-informed in matters of public transport and geography. If not, try to identify a straggler who has been separated from the herd and left to fend for themselves in a strange land. Look out for wide-eyed fear, frantic head movements (in the hope of catching sight of a familiar landmark or a road name) or someone seemingly bewildered by an over-sized map.

If you do detect a lost soul, approach with caution. They may startle easily and react with suspicion or hysterical relief at the offer of help. Speak slowly and articulately – lost tourists tend to have very limited knowledge of the native tongue. Once you've pointed them the right way, follow at a distance to ensure they really have understood your directions.

Your eye-witness report

Fill out the form below and score points along the way.

Your notes

Log any other interesting observations below.

Location and date

Who did this happen to?

M F

How many tourists were lost?

1 ○ 2–5 ○ Lots ○

How many maps did they have?

0 ○ 1 or 2 ○ Lots ○

What were they trying to find?

Land-mark ○ Hotel ○ Street ○ Bar/restaurant ○

What nationality were they?

Place the flag sticker here

Could they speak English?

Yes ○ No ○

Did you take pity on them and show them the sites?

Yes ○

No, I just released them back into the wild ○

How did you score?

Spotted 5 Approach-ed 10 Dir-ections 15 Language 20

TASK Say 'Fromage'

I took a tourist's photo. 25

I was in a tourist's photo. 50

Final score

See a pet that looks like its owner

Award points for:

5 Similar hair

10 Similar build

15 Similar character

20 All of the above

TASK

Matchmaker

Find your perfect pet match.

Wild look-a-life

In the realm of pets that resemble people, dogs reign supreme. No other animal can emulate their owners so convincingly.

Just like their human masters, dogs come in all shades, shapes and sizes, and can sport a variety of hairstyles, such as the perfect poodle perm or the shaggy sheepdog look, not to mention eyebrows, beards and moustaches. But it's not all about aesthetics. Some dogs may even assume their owner's gait or character. From the doleful basset hound, to the chipper border collie and kindly Saint Bernard – some breeds just seem to exude a certain personality. So an Afghan hound might make the perfect companion for a tall, elegant, long-haired blonde lady. And for an overweight, balding football fan who's been around the block a few times? A bulldog, of course.

Spot the dog

A dog may dress like its owner too – and these days that doesn't just mean a neckerchief around the collar. With hoodies, T-shirts, jumpers and even fur coats all available, our streets are turning into a catwalk for canines. For bonus points, spot a dog in fancy dress.

Your eye-witness report

Fill out the form below and score points along the way.

Location and date

📷 **CAPTURE THE MOMENT OR DRAW WHAT YOU SAW** 🖍🖍🖍🖍

Who looked like whom?   Owner like pet ○   Pet like owner ○

How did you score?

Similar hair ☆ 5   Similar build ☆ 10   Similar character ☆ 15   All ☆ 20

TASK Match-maker: I found ...   ... a picture of my perfect pet match ... ☆ 25   ... and now I own that pet. ☆ 50

Your notes

Log any other interesting observations below.

....

....

....

....

....

....

Final score

Spot an act of road rage

Award points for:

 5 Aggressive driving, e.g. tailgating, cutting others off, undertaking

 10 Brawling

 15 Bike rage

 20 Pedestrian rage

TASK

Name and shame

Capture a rage incident on camera and upload it to YouTube.

On the road

Occupying the seat behind the steering wheel of any vehicle can turn a usually sane and reasonable person into a super-angrified *Death Race 2000* contestant with minimal provocation.* Each driver has their own set of rules and without universal agreement on what constitutes good motoring etiquette, or even dangerous driving, the roads become a lawless free-for-all. A typical rager's road commandments include some, if not all, of the following:

None shall converge within a metre of my ride.
None shall go faster than my ride.
None shall go slower than my ride.
None shall stop in front of my ride, including pausing at traffic lights.
None shall touch my ride or look at my ride.
None shall take my parking place. I saw it first.

You can get extra points for spotting those rarer incidents of bike or pedestrian rage, further symptoms of our over-populated and speed-obsessed world. Congested pavements and bike lanes can be just as badly affected by impatient or careless users, and it might not be long before we see fast lanes on pavements and speeding tickets for cyclists.

---

* *Death Race 2000* is a cult action film made in 1975. Set in a dystopian future, it tells the story of a US coast-to-coast race, in which the competitors earn points for each innocent life taken along the way.

CAPTURE THE MOMENT
OR DRAW WHAT YOU SAW

Your eye-witness report

Fill out the form below and score points along the way.

Your notes

Log any other interesting observations below.

Location and date

Which words best describe what you saw?

Shouting	Swearing	Beeping	Flashing
Rude gestures	Tailgating	Cutting up	Cutting off
Undertaking	Swerving	Jumping lights	Speeding
Crawling	Chasing	Hitting	Pushing
Crashing	Apologising	Pulling over	Throwing

How many of the following were involved?

Taxi ◯ Bus ◯ Car ◯ Lorry ◯ Van ◯

Cyclist ◯ Caravan/ trailer ◯ Pedestrian ◯ Emergency vehicle ◯

How did you score?

Aggressive driving 5 Brawling 10 Bike rage 15 Pedestrian rage 20

TASK Name and shame | I caught a road rager on camera ... 25 | ... and I uploaded it to YouTube. 50

Final score

Spot a drunken adventurer

Award points for:

 Jolly japes

 Tanked-up challenges

 Inebriated athletics

20 Superhuman feats

TASK

Home help

Help a drunken adventurer get home.

I'll drink to that ...

Modern life wouldn't be the same without alcohol. It's the social lubricant of choice, releasing our inner daredevil and giving free reign to all things dumb and inadvisable. The catalyst for great nights out and disastrous ones alike, alcohol plays the partner-in-crime to many of our adventures and misadventures, allowing the less daring to let themselves go, and pushing the already daring to go too far.

A drunken adventurer believes him or herself to be adept at all Olympic sports. Swimming, diving, weightlifting, running, climbing or jumping – you name it, a drunken adventurer can, in their eyes, win gold in any number of events. Some feel that their clothes are a hinderance and are best taken off whatever the weather. Total freedom from inhibitions is usually partnered with hearty shouts of self-affirmation, even when some feat has backfired. For a few, the simple task of walking home may be an adventure too far.

As a spotter of one of these escapades, you can be thankful that it's not you this time; for the drunken adventurer, the only reward will be a crashing hangover, patchy memories and the shock of logging on to their social networking sites.

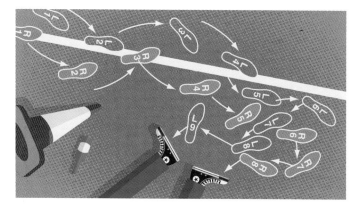

Your eye-witness report

Fill out the form below and score points along the way.

Your notes

Log any other interesting observations below.

Location and date [   ] [   ]

 **CAPTURE THE MOMENT OR DRAW WHAT YOU SAW**

....

....

....

....

....

....

Did the adventurer ... success-◯ ... unsuccess-◯
pull off their stunt ... fully? fully?

How did you score?

Japes ⟨5⟩ Challenges ⟨10⟩ Athletics ⟨15⟩ Super-human ⟨20⟩

TASK Home help | I stopped them from doing something ⟨25⟩ dangerous ... | ... and helped ⟨50⟩ them home.

Final score [   ]

Spot an invasion

Award points for:

5 Nature, e.g. plants, animals or insects

10 Pitch invasion

15 Flash mob

20 Other

TASK

Mob rule

Organise a flash mob.

Space invaders

Not all invasions are of the military kind. They can come in a variety of forms, shapes and sizes. For example, you might see an army of over- or underwhelmed fans gatecrashing a field of play, or a single topless (and sometimes bottomless) trespasser streaking across a games pitch. The street equivalent of a pitch invasion is a flash mob, where seemingly sane and unrelated people suddenly converge on a location, as if spontaneously, in order to create a moment of wonderful madness, like a pillow fight, or to put on a performance of song or dance for sheer amusement, or to advertise something. These invasions can melt away as suddenly as they began.

Rather less amusing is an invasion of animals or insects. You may find your garden plundered by snails, spiders, moles or rabbits, or your house invaded by cockroaches, mice, fleas or moths. With just the right conditions, swarms can come together and get right up in your face, and your nose and your hair. Many creatures love to swarm in the warm, such as flies and bees, midges, ants and locusts. Even the usually lovely ladybird can become a pest when it decides to drop in with thousands of relatives. No matter how lovely a creature is, when they're in their millions you just want them to flock off and die.

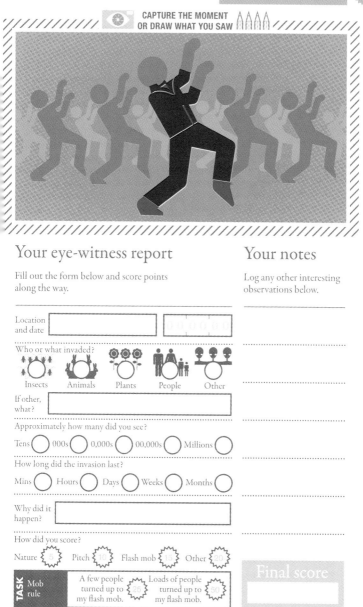

CAPTURE THE MOMENT
OR DRAW WHAT YOU SAW

Your eye-witness report

Fill out the form below and score points along the way.

Your notes

Log any other interesting observations below.

Location and date

Who or what invaded?

Insects · Animals · Plants · People · Other

If other, what?

Approximately how many did you see?

Tens ○ · 000s ○ · 0,000s ○ · 00,000s ○ · Millions ○

How long did the invasion last?

Mins ○ · Hours ○ · Days ○ · Weeks ○ · Months ○

Why did it happen?

How did you score?

Nature ☆5 · Pitch ☆10 · Flash mob ☆15 · Other ☆20

TASK Mob rule · A few people turned up to my flash mob. ☆25 · Loads of people turned up to my flash mob. ☆50

Final score

Spot someone you know on the news

Award points for:

 5 Someone you know in a TV audience

 10 Someone you know on the radio

 15 Someone you know on a TV show

 20 Someone you know on the news

TASK

Newsflash!

Get into the background of a live news report. Flashing is optional but not encouraged.

News worthy?

The news is a sobering affair which, from time to time, can be livened up by seeing someone you know on screen. Hopefully your family member, friend or acquaintances' appearance won't be to do with a crime or disaster. There are plenty of other ways to get on there ...

Interviews: See someone you know talk about their charity work, voice their opinions about some government announcement or complain about the rising dog poo problem in their neighbourhood.

Quirky stories: Editors like the news to end on an upbeat story, so keep an eye out for your friend and her gymnastic gerbils.

Gatecrash: There's always the possibility of you knowing that idiot jumping around behind the reporter in a live broadcast.

If there's no one you know that's newsworthy, you might still be lucky enough to spot an acquaintance on a game or talent show, or in a crowd or studio audience. And if you still can't spot anyone you know, listen out for them instead. Radio broadcasters love to make contact with their audience, in the form of interviews, dedications, phone-ins and anecdotes.

CAPTURE THE MOMENT
OR DRAW WHAT YOU SAW

SOMEONE YOU KNOW

BREAKING NEWS

07:03

Your eye-witness report

Fill out the form below and score points along the way.

Location and date	

Who did you see or hear?

	TV Radio
Name of show?	◯ ◯

What kind of broadcast was it?

Local ◯ Regional ◯ National ◯ Worldwide ◯

What were they doing?

Rate their performance

So bad it was good | Pretty bad | Not great | Pretty good | Great! | Amazing!

◯ ◯ ◯ ◯ ◯ ◯

How did you score?

TV audience ⟡ 5 | Radio ⟡ 10 | TV show ⟡ 15 | On the news ⟡ 20

TASK Newsflash! I was in the background of a ⟡ 25 ... and behaved like an idiot. ⟡ 50

Your notes

Log any other interesting observations below.

Final score

Spot a sporting blunder (or wonder)

Award points for:

 5 Embarrassing or accidental

 10 Idiotic or on purpose

15 Bizarre or spectacular

20 A record-breaking achievement

TASK

Animal antics

Spot an animal intruder in a sports competition.

Sporting chance

It takes hard work and dedication to master a sport, and even then there's no guarantee you won't make an arse of yourself. Sheer luck or skill can produce a sporting wonder, but there are many more ways to cock up. Here is a handful to look out for …

Own goal: A move/mistake that allows the opposition to score/win.
Over-confidence: This could be someone who thinks they've scored or won when they haven't, or who goofs up a pointless flashy move.
Sheer ineptitude: A golden opportunity is inexplicably squandered and you wonder if you couldn't have done better yourself.
Clothes/equipment malfunctions: Look out for breakages, rips, tears, and the odd embarrassing flash.
Bad loser: Tears, tantrums, throwing, pushing and storming off.
Bad winner: Competitors who perform mystifying or cringeworthy routines or who mess up their over-jubilant acrobatics.
Cheating: A sneaky nudge of the ball, a blatant dive, a faked injury, a sly push, a fixed match, a corrupt official or equipment sabotage.
Mascot mayhem: In those over-sized costumes, it's easy to run into things, fall over or get in the way of play. One ice hockey mascot even managed to set himself on fire.

CAPTURE THE MOMENT
OR DRAW WHAT YOU SAW

Your eye-witness report

Fill out the form below and score points along the way.

Location and date [ ] [0 0 0 0 0]

Type of sport [ ]

Which words best describe what you saw?

Acrobatics	Fluke	Embarrassing	Ambitious
Spectacular	Spill	Fall	Break
Record-breaking	Foolhardy	Accidental	Idiotic
Genius	Showing off	Hit	Miss
Cheating	Tantrum	Invasion	Slapstick
Unlucky	Lucky	Nudity	Acting

What malfunctioned?

Clothing ( )   Equipment ( )   Nature ( )   People ( )

How did you score?

Cringy/Accident **5**   Idiotic/deliberate **10**   Bizarre/amazing **15**   Record-breaking **20**

TASK Animal antics   I saw an animal stop to take a look. **25**   I saw an animal get involved. **50**

Your notes

Log any other interesting observations below.

Final score

[ ]

See a multiple rainbow

Award points for:

5 A secondary rainbow

10 More than two rainbows

15 A twinned or reflected rainbow

20 Other rainbow phenomena

TASK

Colouring in

Make your own rainbow using any of the following: water, a glass, a CD, a mirror, a hose, a torch, the sun.

Way up high ...

It is always a delight to see a rainbow, one of nature's most beautiful light shows, and the best time to spot one is when it's been raining and the sky is still dark with rain clouds, but there is also clear sky and low sunlight. A rainbow will always appear opposite the sun, as it is formed by light being reflected in the raindrops.

When you've spotted one, look above it, because somewhere over the rainbow may, in fact, be another rainbow. Secondary rainbows are caused by a double reflection of light within the raindrops and they're usually fainter than the primary, which can make them hard to spot. The colours appear in reverse order too, with violet on the outer edge through to red on the inside. The darker patch of unlit sky between the primary and secondary rainbows is called Alexander's band.

If you're really lucky, you could also see ...

... a tertiary or quaternary rainbow, or a twinned one (two rainbows splitting from a single base), or a reflected one (caused by sunlight being reflected in still water). And you might find the whole multiple-rainbow experience as overwhelming as Paul 'Bear' Vasquez.*

* Check out his home video on YouTube: http://goo.gl/qQc1

Your eye-witness report

Fill out the form below and score points along the way.

| Location and date | | |

CAPTURE THE MOMENT
OR DRAW WHAT YOU SAW

How did you score?

Secondary ⭐ 5   3+ ⭐ 10   Twinned/ reflected ⭐ 15   Other ⭐ 20

TASK Colouring in   I made a rainbow. ⭐ 25   I made multiple rainbows. ⭐ 50

Your notes

Log any other interesting observations below.

....

....

....

....

....

....

Final score

Spot a Christmas overdose

Award points for:

 5 A blowout or blow up, e.g. a feast that requires intervals, an argument

 10 A Scrooge, i.e. someone who ignores or avoids Christmas

15 A bad Santa

20 Over-the-top illuminations/ decorations

TASK

Recycled Christmas

Waste nothing at Christmas by recycling your leftovers, your cards and your unwanted gifts.

Do They Know It's Christmas?

Christmas is a joyful time, but you can definitely have too much of a good thing. Whether it's an overdose of food, family or sheer expense, some people are just a bit relieved to get it over with, while others go out of the way to pretend it's not happening at all.

Look out for Santas who have run out of Christmas cheer, who have heard those hits of yesteryear just once or a thousand times too often, whose knees are aching with the weight of fidgety, ungrateful children, some of whom pull his beard, pee on his lap or puke their chocolate-stuffed guts up all over the grotto. You might spot a Santa who was never right in the first place, thin and mean-looking, with a crap beard and a badly made costume.

Perhaps you'll come across one of those houses that has been transformed into a garish light show of twinkle and tat. A small country could be powered on the electricity needed to illuminate some light-laden homes and gardens. And if you peer into enough windows, you're bound to spot an arsonist's dream: a room lined with tinsel and lametta, and struggling to contain some overloaded glittering giant in the corner that once was a tree.

CAPTURE THE MOMENT
OR DRAW WHAT YOU SAW

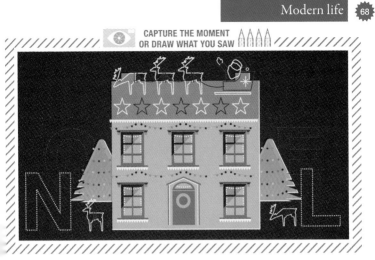

Your eye-witness report

Fill out the form below and score points along the way.

Your notes

Log any other interesting observations below.

Location and date

Who was the victim(s)?

○ ○ ○ ○ ○ ○ ○ ○ ○ ○

What did you witness an overdose of?

Xmas cheer ○ Presents ○ Food ○ Alcohol ○

Xmas songs ○ Decorations ○ TV ○ Family ○

What else did you see?

Arguments ○ Tastless-ness ○ Mean-spiritedness ○ Tears ○

Ungrateful-ness ○ Drunken-ness ○ Exhaustion ○ Sick ○

How did you score?

Blowout/blow up 5 Scrooge 10 Bad Santa 15 OTT decorations 20

TASK Recycled Xmas We ate all the food ... 25 ... and sold, returned or gave away all the unwanted presents. 50

Final score

Spot the next big thing

Award points for:

5 A friend trend

10 A local fad

15 A national craze

20 A global phenomenon

TASK

Trendsetter

Initiate the
next big thing.

Vogue

Trends are life-invading phenomena that emerge seemingly from nowhere and last until the next big thing comes along or collective boredom kicks in. And thanks to the power of the media, modern life is obsessed with them.

Fashion trends are usually set by celebrities, who are themselves trends that come and go, depending on what they're doing, who they're dating and what they're wearing. With swift developments in technology, a game-changing device will shine brightly until the launch of game changer 2.0. And you'll need these new technologies to spot an incoming trend, for they will increasingly give you unlimited access to everyone and everything going on everywhere.

The Internet can produce and disseminate a trend in the blink of an eye. Peruse all social networks designed to promote love affairs among people you know and people you don't. Predict a topical twitter account on the back of a hot topic and keep an eye out for potential memes, those short-lived Internet sensations that often take the form of a new dance craze. Keep your ear to the ground and your finger on the pulse, as people can lose Pinterest in an Instagram.

CAPTURE THE MOMENT
OR DRAW WHAT YOU SAW

Your eye-witness report

Fill out the form below and score points along the way.

Your notes

Log any other interesting observations below.

Location and date

I BELIEVE **THE NEXT BIG THING** IS GOING TO BE ...

Did it happen?

Hairstyle: .... Yes ◯ No ◯

Fashion: .... Yes ◯ No ◯

Social: .... Yes ◯ No ◯

Political: .... Yes ◯ No ◯

Cultural: .... Yes ◯ No ◯

Other: .... Yes ◯ No ◯

How did you score?

Friend trend 5   Local fad 10   National craze 15   Global phenomenon 20

TASK I started a trend ...   ... but no one followed it. 25   ... and people followed it. 50

Final score

Spot the ultimate epic win and fail

Award points for:

5 Designed to fail,
   e.g. a tool or product fail

10 Deserved to fail, e.g. downright
   stupidity, lack of skill

15 Destined to fail,
   e.g. bad luck, bad timing

20 A spectacular cock-up

TASK

Ultimate epic win

Spot a moment of spectacular good luck or skill, the more unexpected the better.

Epic failure is an option

Our journey through life is punctuated with unforgettable moments, from euphoric highs to depressing lows, with a handful of epic tales and fails dotted in between. Hopefully the highs dominate, the lows are fleeting and the fails are someone else's and caught on camera.

Everything we do can be a success or a failure, from eating and walking, to bolder endeavours, like parking a car or baking a cake. This book is full of potential fails, but the list is endless. It's everyday actions, such as sitting down or picking something up, that make for the most hilarious fails. If someone attempts something difficult and fails, the result is less likely to amuse, unless they fail in spectacular fashion.

Professionals and amateurs, manufacturers and consumers, children and animals – no one is immune from an epic fail. All it takes is a lack of skill, a lapse in concentration, a moment of madness or a stroke of bad luck for something which should be easy to go wrong. Conversely, a stroke of good luck or genius might result in something seemingly impossible to succeed. Epic fails and wins can come at any time, in any place, from anywhere, so be prepared. Always have a camera to hand and, just to be on the safe side, film every moment of your life 24/7.

Your eye-witness report

Fill out the form below and score points along the way.

Location and date [   ] [   ]

.... Place a photo, draw or ....
write about the event
you witnessed here

EPIC FAIL/WIN

Just when you thought you'd seen everything ...

How did you score?

Designed to fail {5} Deserved to fail {10} Destined to fail {15} Amazing cock-up {20}

TASK Ultimate epic win | I saw someone or something produce an epic win. {25} | I produced an epic win. {50}

Your notes

Log any other interesting observations below.

....

....

....

....

....

....

Final score

[   ]

APPENDIX

You've reached the final part of the book, where you can take stock of the things you've seen along your modern-day spotting journey.

Enter your scores for each spot in the **YOUR TOTALS** section on the following pages. Once you've added up the points for all your spots so far, find out which title and merit you've achieved.

If there are any other things you've spotted along the way that weren't featured in the book, then you can enter them in the extra pages provided.

You'll also find links to the website, where you can upload the things you've spotted and share your stories.

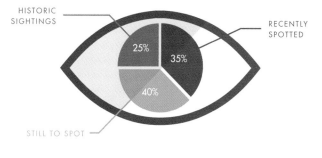

HISTORIC SIGHTINGS

RECENTLY SPOTTED

25%

35%

40%

STILL TO SPOT

YOUR TOTALS

	DATE		TOTALS
1		Spot something left on the roof of a car	
2		Spot an escaped animal	
3		Spot an unusual-shaped cloud	
4		See the face of Jesus in your soup	
5		Spot a commuter miss their stop	
6		Spot an amusing place name	
7		Spot a photo bombing	
8		Spot a movie mistake	
9		Spot a wild animal using public transport	
10		Spot a modern-day shooting star	
11		Spot someone in a time warp	

	DATE		TOTALS
12		Spot a living statue on a break	
13		Spot a wardrobe malfunction	
14		Spot an invisible foe attack	
15		Spot someone using unusual transport	
16		Spot an amusing news headline	
17		Spot a thieving seagull	
18		Spot an embarrassed parent	
19		See your name on a gravestone	
20		Spot a dancing plastic bag	
21		Spot an awkward date	
22		Spot an amusingly shaped vegetable	
23		Spot an amusing auto-correction	
24		Spot something unusual on a bus shelter	
25		Spot a public typo	
26		Spot a food malfunction	
27		Spot interesting facial hair	
28		Spot a celebrity lookalike	
29		See a face in an everyday place	
30		Spot a competitive parent	
31		Spot something unusual on Google Street View	
32		Spot a bird-poo victim	

	DATE		**TOTALS**
33		Spot a dropped photo	
34		Spot someone with techno rage	
35		Spot an inappropriate T-shirt	
36		Spot a pigeon with one foot	
37		Spot a battle against the wind	
38		Spot a prank	
39		Spot something you've dreamt about	
40		Spot a bad hair day	
41		Spot a good deed	
42		Spot the inexplicable	
43		Spot an identical or odd couple	
44		Spot an optical illusion	
45		Spot a public meltdown	
46		Spot an 'X' in the sky made by vapour trails	
47		Spot a moment of pure slapstick	
48		Spot a film set in action	
49		Spot a cat with a moustache	
50		See a lightning strike	
51		Spot lost treasure	
52		Spot someone's double	
53		Spot a memorable wedding moment	

	DATE			TOTALS
54		Spot someone incognito		
55		Spot something hanging on overhead wires		
56		Spot a criminal act (and someone thwarting it)		
57		Spot someone on their way to a fancy-dress party		
58		Spot a bad tattoo		
59		Spot someone go against the flow		
60		Spot a lost tourist		
61		See a pet that looks like its owner		
62		Spot an act of road rage		
63		Spot a drunken adventurer		
64		Spot an invasion		
65		Spot someone you know on the news		
66		Spot a sporting blunder (or wonder)		
67		See a multiple rainbow		
68		Spot a Christmas overdose		
69		Spot the next big thing		
70		Spot the ultimate epic win and fail		

	YOUR OVERALL TOTAL	

As you work through the list of spots, you will earn *Modern Day Spotter's Guide* titles in honour of your achievements. The more you things you spot, the greater the title.

The points you've been accumulating will count here too. In recognition of the extra effort you may have put in to gain the rarest spots and to complete the tasks, you can add a Bronze, Silver or Gold merit, depending on your overall points total at that stage. For example, if you had seen 21 things on the list, and had a points total of 525, you would earn the title of See Farer Bronze.

As you work your way up the honours list, visit the *Modern Day Spotter's Guide* website to enter your current status and to see how others are faring.

5 THINGS SPOTTED:
SEE CADET

You have achieved the title of See Cadet.
Welcome to the world of modern-day spotting.
We hope you're enjoying the view.

See Cadet Bronze: 125–189 points
See Cadet Silver: 190–249 points
See Cadet Gold: 250–500 points

15 THINGS SPOTTED:
SEE FARER

You have earned the honour of See Farer.
You've made a great start to your modern-day
spotting career. Keep up the good work.

See Farer Bronze: 350–674 points
See Farer Silver: 675–999 points
See Farer Gold: 1000–1500 points

25 THINGS SPOTTED:
SIGHT SEERER

You are now a Sightseer.
Keep spying with your little eyes.
The only way is up.

Sight Seer Bronze: 575–899 points
Sight Seer Silver: 900–1299 points
Sight Seer Gold: 1300–2500 points

40 THINGS SPOTTED:
SPY MASTER

You have been awarded Spy Master.
Congratulations! Well over half the
list has been completed.

Spy Master Bronze: 900–1499 points
Spy Master Silver: 1500–2099 points
Spy Master Gold: 2100–4000 points

55 THINGS SPOTTED:
HAWK EYE

You have earned the title of Hawk Eye.
You're well on your way to achieving legendary
status in the Modern Day Spotter's world.

Hawk Eye Bronze: 1250–1999 points
Hawk Eye Silver: 2000–2874 points
Hawk Eye Gold: 2875–5500 points

65+ THINGS SPOTTED:
EAGLE EYE

You have reached the top class of Eagle Eye.
Over 65 things spotted is an amazing achievement.
Long may you continue to spot such anecdotal
incidents, everyday oddities and epic fails.

Eagle Eye Bronze: 1475–2399 points
Eagle Eye Silver: 2400–3399 points
Eagle Eye Gold: 3400–7000 points

YOUR SPOTS

It's impossible to cover every interesting eventuality that you may spot as you journey through life, but hopefully this book gives an all-round taster of the kind of small wonders and curiosities the world has to offer if you only open your eyes.

If you think there's something really obvious that we've missed, then enter your own spots in the following extra pages, with a few notes on what you saw.

If you think your idea is good enough to be in this book and you would like it to be considered for any future projects, then please send it to the author and publisher via the website: www.spottersguide.co.uk

Your eye-witness report

Fill out the form below and score points
along the way.

Location
and date | | 0 0 0 0 0

CAPTURE THE MOMENT
OR DRAW WHAT YOU SAW

Your notes

Log any other interesting
observations below.

....

....

....

....

....

....

Your eye-witness report

Fill out the form below and score points
along the way.

Location
and date | | 0 0 0 0 0

CAPTURE THE MOMENT
OR DRAW WHAT YOU SAW

Your notes

Log any other interesting
observations below.

....

....

....

....

....

....

Your eye-witness report

Fill out the form below and score points along the way.

Location and date

CAPTURE THE MOMENT
OR DRAW WHAT YOU SAW

Your notes

Log any other interesting observations below.

....

....

....

....

....

....

Your eye-witness report

Fill out the form below and score points along the way.

Location and date

CAPTURE THE MOMENT
OR DRAW WHAT YOU SAW

Your notes

Log any other interesting observations below.

....

....

....

....

....

....

The website of the book:

www.spottersguide.co.uk

Facebook:

www.facebook.com/RichardHorneDesign
www.facebook.com/theMDSGbook

The website of the author:

www.elhorno.co.uk

Twitter:

@elhorno – Richard Horne
Hashtag: #MDSG

The website of the publisher – Square Peg, Random House:

www.vintage-books.co.uk

THANK YOU

ACKNOWLEDGEMENTS

Firstly, a huge thank you to Helen Szirtes for her time, patience, editing skills and for planting the seed of the idea in the first place. Thank you for transforming my clunky sentences and rearranging my errant words. This book wouldn't be the same without you.

Thank you to Rosemary Davidson for being so enthusiastic about my unusual projects and for spotting the potential in this idea.

Thanks to the following for their stories and input that have helped shape this book: Philippa Milnes Smith, Ele Fountain, Jane Horne, Ruby Harrison, Christine and Neville Horne, Clarissa Upchurch, George Szirtes, Tom Szirtes, Rob Ellis, Rob Hackett, Paramjit Virdee, The *Norwich Evening News* and the *Eastern Daily Press*, Jo Stafford, Vicki Johnson, Hayley, Neil and Daisy Gosling, Su Owen, David Drake, Joanna Millington, Paul Flack, Kim Haddock, Iain Young, Dom Bellingham, Henry Layte and *the Book Hive*, Simon

Rhodes, Cian McCourt, The entertaining and inspirational tweets by @PresentCorrect, House cafe and the Window coffee shop for the enlightening coffee breaks.

An honoury mention to those that like to help out, namely: Ryan Watts, Caroline Sykes, Sammy Merry, Libby Ostle Bowker, Becky Webb, Stephen Laverick, Beck Illsley, Karly Ellis, Zoe Thomas, Sophia Colley, Paul Nash, Tim Moss, Jennie Walker, Isabella Pereira, Neil Tweddle, Nick Stone, Sarah Bays and Lee Smith of the *Norwich Frame Workshop*. Thank you. Thank you.

Finally, a big thank you to the cities of London and Norwich for providing much of the inspiration for the spots in this book. There's nowt so funny as folk.

ABOUT THE AUTHOR

Richard Horne is a graphic designer, illustrator, author, screen and gocco printer. He has written, illustrated and designed six other books, five in the popular *101 Things To Do* series and *A is for Armageddon*, an illustrated catalogue of disasters. He also illustrated the bestselling book, *The Dangerous Book for Boys*, winner of the 2007 book of the year at the British Book Awards.

He lives in Norwich, UK.